LIFESAVING

The Story of the Royal Life Saving Society

THE FIRST 100 YEARS

LIFESAVING

The Story of the Royal Life Saving Society

THE FIRST 100 YEARS

Ronald Pearsall

DAVID & CHARLES
Newton Abbot London

FRONTISPIECE:
Lifeguards devoting their time
in a practice rescue

ACKNOWLEDGEMENTS

Grateful thanks to all the many contributors

British Library Cataloguing in Publication Data

Pearsall, Ronald
Lifesaving: the story of The Royal Life Saving Society:
the first 100 years.
1. Great Britain. Life Saving Organisation.
Royal Life Saving Society, history
I. Title
363.14

ISBN 0 – 7153 – 9867 – 9

Typeset and designed by John Youé
using a Macintosh system
and printed in Portugal by Resopal
for David & Charles plc
Brunel House Newton Abbot Devon

Contents

Foreword

THE ROYAL LIFE SAVING SOCIETY COMMONWEALTH PRESIDENT
His Royal Highness Prince Michael of Kent
(Portrait by George A. Weymouth)

This book provides a fascinating background to the growth of our Society. Born of a need identified by its Victorian founders, it was based on an ideal described in its motto: 'Whomsoever you see in distress, recognise in him a fellow man.' The Society has continued to fulfil a vital role in life saving and over its first hundred years its work has helped millions in more than fifty countries.

Much of the information for this book has had to be drawn from sources available in the United Kingdom, where the Society originated. The essence and heart of the Society is the family ethos of our Commonwealth. Every country concerned has worked ceaselessly towards reducing the number of people drowned. In a matter of moments a peaceful swim or an everyday activity cantered by the nightmare of a tragic and horrifying death.

It is a daunting task to cover adequately one hundred years of service to the community in a single volume without it becoming too unwieldy; and, for this reason, the chapters on 'Drowning Facts and Figures' and 'The Lifeguard's Tale' relate only to the United Kingdom Branch. 'Drowning Facts and Figures' illustrates clearly the pattern of improvement common to all Member Branches and it is encouraging to note how that follows wherever life saving work is initiated.

'The Lifeguard's Tale' is devoted to the Lifeguard Corps - now RLSS Lifeguards - here in the United Kingdom and to the valuable community service they provide in promoting safer aquatic activity. There are examples to be drawn from beyond our shores, too. They include the professionalism of the voluntary lifeguard units in Canada; the sharing of responsibility in Australia and New Zealand with the Surf Life Saving Associations; and the development of lifeguarding services in Barbados, Bermuda, Sierra Leone, Sri Lanka and Trinidad & Tobago. Accounts of those exploits could themselves fill another volume.

The achievements of the first hundred years of the Royal Life Saving Society form a sure foundation for the challenges of the future.

Michael

HRH Prince Michael of Kent

Introduction

Water is not a natural environment for mankind. If it were, we would be equipped with flippers and a greater lung capacity. Water can be hostile, and from earliest times man realised the need to survive in water and invent rescue techniques. It is known that mouth-to-mouth resuscitation and cardiac massage were known and practised from ancient times.

But it was a long time before the appearance of the Swimmers' Life Saving Society, formed in 1891 by William Henry, an excellent swimmer. This society was later renamed the Royal Life Saving Society. And with its centenary in 1991 it is time to give it its due deserts. Its motto is *Quemcunque Miserum Videris Hominem Scias* ('Whomsoever you see in distress recognise in him a fellow man'). The work of the society had royal patronage and expanded rapidly. In 1964, Queen Elizabeth — who had gained the society's Intermediate Certificate in 1938 — approved the use of the Royal Crown with the society's badge.

Throughout the present century the Royal Family has fully supported the Royal Life Saving Society, none more so than Lord Louis Mountbatten, commemorated by Mountbatten House, the headquarters of the Royal Life Saving Society UK and Commonwealth Headquarters, and opened in 1981 by Her Majesty Queen Elizabeth, the Queen Mother.

Today, with watersports of all kinds so common, the need for committed and professionally trained lifesavers is greater than ever, to rescue those members of the public who may be silly, absent-minded, careless, egotistical — or again, just unfortunate. Many a sensible person has come to grief in water through no fault of his or her own.

The Royal Life Saving Society has done sterling work in the UK and throughout the Commonwealth, where conditions are so different from those in Britain. No one can say how many have been saved from drowning, not only by rescue but by instruction, by comprehensive series of handbooks, guides, and videos, and by the tuition imparted in schools and to youth and adult groups of all kinds. The society is not subsidised; the members are volunteers. Half a million people are involved in some way in the society's work in the UK alone, and millions more in the Commonwealth counties, where new branches are constantly being formed.

This book is a tribute, a history of the society, and a vivid and fascinating study of all aspects of lifesaving.

If general readers begin to realise that water can be dangerous and not something provided by providence for cups of tea and the leisure industry then this book will be worthwhile.

1891-1910

The Springboard Years

In the 1880s swimming was incredibly popular, with hundreds of well-supported clubs; professional swimmers were able to make a good living by exhibiting their skills, one of which was remaining underwater in a tank on a music-hall stage for nearly five minutes. As in all sports of the time there was a clear division between amateurs and professionals.

It occurred to some of the more thoughtful swimmers that not much attention was being paid to 'the most essential feature of their art', rescuing persons in danger of drowning by swimming to their relief. Some clubs did, but there was little practice and although there were competitions these were carried out unsystematically and on a local level.

In 1887 the Royal Humane Society was approached by William Henry, a talented swimmer, and asked to undertake the instruction, using its own organisation and staff. There was little interest in the proposal, but he and his friend Archibald Sinclair followed it up with a letter, setting forth a scheme for forming classes of instruction in the most approved methods of lifesaving. The following day the secretary of the Royal Humane Society wrote back to say that the society had already instituted a prize for swimming, and that 'the committee can do no more without neglecting the legitimate work of the society.'

Henry and Sinclair considered the matter, and the Amateur Swimming Association was approached, and appointed a committee, which on 11 May 1889 made its report. It said that a central committee of seven should be appointed, that classes should be held, local arrangements being made by swimming clubs in the locality, and that lecturers should be provided by the committee. Demonstrations of restoring the apparently drowned would be carried out, and that societies and schools would be brought into the scheme.

Clubs would be asked to print lifesaving rules in their lists of fixtures, and give demonstrations of rescue and restoration at their competitions and demonstrations. The first step would be to hold a preliminary meeting at a 'good bath', with demonstrations of rescue work by swimmers, and restoration of a person apparently drowned, by a qualified medical practitioner. All swimming clubs would be circularised to keep them informed of these proposals. The expense of lifesaving classes would be met by the clubs, by the central committee, by subscriptions, and by grants from the Amateur Swimming Association, if necessary.

All very sensible and straightforward. But nothing further was done.

A good living was to be made by remaining underwater in a tank on a music-hall stage. Especially if a well-rounded lady!

BREATHING FOR PLEASURE OR PROFIT?

Entertainment can come in a variety of forms. During the last years of the nineteenth century there was one in particular that must have alarmed doctors in the music-hall audiences. This was the popular amusement of staying underwater. This form of entertainment is, of course, known today when sleight-of-hand operators rid themselves of chains and other encumbrances whilst underwater, but it is not pursued with the same intensity as it was in the 1890s.

The basic premise of the music-hall stunt was immersion in a transparent tank, and the practitioners were mostly women. There was a reason for this. The music-hall was one of the few places where men could see women in a state of partial undress, and a woman in swimming garb, even the voluminous dress of the time, was the *non plus ultra.*

As in all such acts, there was a lead-up, during which the performer did certain tasks underwater, taking breaths between each activity. These included undressing under water, writing on slate, sewing, eating grapes, and drinking from a bottle. Each of these took less than a minute, and relied for their effect on novelty rather than physical prowess. But what the audience paid to see was the feat of remaining beneath water for a long time, and the greatest practitioner of the time was Miss Elise Wallenda, who on 14 December 1899

continued overleaf

continued

remained underwater for 4min 45.4sec.

Although pearl-fishers have the ability to remain underwater for long periods, spectators are inclined to overestimate the time, and nearly five minutes is incredible. Medical advisers to the Amateur Swimming Association advised that a minute was quite sufficient for underwater swimming without aids, and any further time spent underwater could wreak irreparable damage. One daring doctor-swimmer decided to see what would happen if he remained underwater for a longer period. He found that he became sanguine and unconcerned, not caring whether or not he came up to the surface to breathe. Fortunately he had the sense to realise that he was behaving irrationally, so did ascend to the surface and presumably survived without ill effect.

Miss Elise Wallenda was the daughter of a German dog-trainer, born in Mayence, and from an early age swam in the Rhine with her sisters, where they were known, not surprisingly as the 'Rhine Maidens.' Elise and her sisters were fond of gymnastics, and in 1889 they decided to bring their talents to the notice of the British music-hall audience, though there was no question that Elise, aged eighteen, was the star of the troupe.

The tank she used was 10ft

continued on page 12

The Amateur Swimming Association traces its ancestry from the Associated Metropolitan Swimming Clubs formed in 1869, and it had several titles in subsequent years. A contemporary swimmer, R. P. Watson declared in his memoirs of 1899 that 'round this tempest-tossed institution might be written a remarkable story.' Certainly few had heard of the organisation, whatever name it was travelling under, up to 1877, where there was still no ruling body; and an annual yearbook was not published until 1893. The reluctance to participate in the scheme proposed by Henry and Sinclair may have been due to the fact that there was simply no appropriate structure for arranging the details.

Nevertheless Henry and Sinclair were not deterred and on 3 January 1891 there was a meeting at Anderton's Hotel, London, of seven persons interested in everything that pertained to swimming. This was the nucleus of the worldwide organisation that was soon to be the pre-eminent lifesaving society. The men at this

8 Bayley Street, London, where William Henry lived and which was an early headquarters of the RLSS. It is now occupied by the National Council for Voluntary Organisations – quite appropriate

In the early years of swimming pools – this hand-coloured print depicts a French swimming pool of 1872 – there were many ways of being taught to swim, some better than others!

meeting were Henry himself; Archibald Sinclair; H. Hewitt Griffin; F.W. Moses; E.W. Stafford; W. Brickett; C. Val Hunter. The meeting was attended by about sixty people. A committee of twelve, all swimmers, was appointed to draw up rules, and it was resolved to term the society the Swimmers' Life Saving Society.

At this stage, the two most important personages were William Henry and Archibald Sinclair. William Henry was the son of Joseph Nawrocki, a Pole, and Elizabeth, nee Amour, an Englishwoman, and was born on 28 June 1859 in London and christened at St Pancras parish church. After a long residence in Russia, the family returned to England in 1877 whereupon William Henry Nawrocki decided to drop his surname because of the difficulty English people found in pronouncing it. Later, on 14 March 1896, he formally took the surname Henry by deed poll.

There is no doubt that William Henry was one of the most important swimmers of his day. In 1883 he was runner-up in the English 500yd Championship, in 1887 runner-up in the English 220yd Championship, in 1888 he was English Saltwater Champion and runner-up in 1890. At a time when long-distance swimming was the most newsworthy he became renowned even

Advertisers saw a good opportunity to promote their wares through swimming. Elliman's Embrocation was one of the more relevant

USE ELLIMAN'S FOR CRAMP.

outside swimming circles when he won the English Long Distance Championship in 1890. This took place along a five-to-six-mile stretch of the River Thames, and finished up off the Houses of Parliament. In 1887, 1888, 1889, 1890 and 1893 he was third in the English Plunging (Diving) Championship, and in 1890 and 1892 he played water polo for England.

On a visit to Germany in 1896 on behalf of the society he found out that the European Championship was being held at Frankfort-on-Maine. Without further ado he borrowed a swimming costume, entered, and won the 100m. He was also Scientific Swimming Champion in 1896, 1899, 1900 and 1901, and won the Life Saving Championship at the World Championship in Paris in 1900.

Archibald Sinclair was a minor figure compared with Henry. He was a journalist, born about 1866, and he had been on the staff of *The Sportsman* and was a sub-editor of the sporting newspaper *The Referee.*

The title of the Swimmers' Life Saving Society was changed to the Life Saving Society. On 25 May 1891 the first lecture was delivered at the Polytechnic Institute in London by Sir Andrew Clark, FRCS. Sir Andrew Clark was one of the most famous medical men of his age, born in 1826, and settling in London in 1854 where his skill in the treatment of diseases affecting the respiratory, renal, and digestive organs made him renowned. Amongst his patients was the novelist George Eliot and the Prime Minister, William Gladstone. The newly fledged society could not have wished for a more eminent person to give credence to the society, though Sir Andrew died soon afterwards, in 1893.

Many meetings were held in 1891, and there were numerous demonstrations at club entertainments. However, great difficulty was found in carrying out the instructions systematically or

continued from page 10

long and 2 ft 4in wide, with the water level at 4ft 4in. The back and the bottom of the tank were made of iron, and the sides and the front were of thick glass. So that there could be no accusations of fraud there were professional observers, including William Henry.

Before she went underwater Miss Wallenda took one long and deep inspiration, then settled down in the bottom of the tank lying on her left side facing the audience, her head resting on her left hand, her body and legs straight with the feet crossed. The observers called out the time each minute. Just before the 3min mark a small bubble of air rose to the surface, and at 3 min 30 sec the bubbles became frequent and at 4min the bubbles ascended in a stream. At 4min 15sec Miss Wallenda seemed to show signs of distress, and William Henry sent her sister to her. The sister was waved away. At the 4min 36sec mark a large bubble escaped from her mouth, and a few seconds later she tried to rise, placing her hand on the bottom of the tank but failing to get any leverage. As she slipped, the watchers ran forward and brought her to the surface.

She threw her head back, opened her mouth wide, and tried to inhale, but was unable to do so until slight pressure was applied to her lower ribs. She speedily gained control of her breathing and within half a minute of leaving the tank she was bowing to the cheering spectators.

During the performance, it

continued opposite

uniformly, and although the instructions of the Royal Humane Society were used as a basis for resuscitation, rescue methods had to be worked out from scratch as those employed by the various clubs in isolation proved too crude or unworkable.

Methods had to be easily understood by the general public, and the instruction had to be made attractive so that the interest would be retained. It was decided to present rescue techniques in the form of drill movements and three books were taken as primers — the *British Army Drill Book,* the manual of the Medical Staff Corps (later the Royal Army Medical Corps), and Lieutenant Torkington's *Swimming Drill.* A report was written based on information gleaned from these books, but before it was studied a number of illustrated articles explaining a system of drill was published in the *North British Daily Mail.* This drill had been evolved by William Wilson, and had been practised in Glasgow on a competitive basis, with Wilson himself awarding prizes.

The main aim of the Life Saving Society was to raise swimming

continued

was noted, the chest was perfectly still, but the abdomen was constantly moving up and down; as the abdomen fell the throat became distended, and vice versa.

It was believed by many that her feat was solely due to her lung capacity, but a spirometer was brought and it was found that her lung capacity was 132cu in of air, far below that of her sisters who could not stay underwater longer than 2min and hardly more than a third of the lung capacity of one of the observers who confessed that at times he had tried to 'hang on' whilst 'plunging' and had had difficulty in holding his breath longer than a minute.

Miss Wallenda had a chest measurement of 27in deflated, 31in fully inflated. Her height was 4ft 9in, her weight 6st 7lb. There were many learned theories regarding her undoubted abilities. The 'amount of tissue aerated by the blood . . . the supply of air in proportion to her size.' But most agreed that there were 'abstruse points yet to be decided.'

It is not known what became of Miss Wallenda, and whether her curious way of earning a living resulted in a premature death. She was certainly a nine-day wonder. A previous record-holder had claimed five minutes, but he had had access to a diving-bell and his claim was contemptuously dismissed. But even at the time swimming authorities and experts pointed

continued overleaf

Land drill was a popular discipline amongst the early lifesavers

continued

out the extreme dangers of underwater practice, so much so that one star, 'Professor' James Finney had himself medically examined after thirteen years at his underwater profession and publicised the results in a Sunday paper.

But during this time Professor Finney had only averaged between 3min and 3min 15sec, and no doubt after Miss Wallenda's achievement he must have found it difficult to get top billing, especially at the Alhambra Theatre, Leicester Square, where Miss Wallenda had enjoyed her greatest and perhaps ultimate success.

above the level of a competitive sport. Many club members imagined that the holding of races was sufficient to prepare rescuers, but many speed swimmers had found that their skills were of little use in lifesaving. Many could swim out to a 'casualty' but were quite unable to bring the victim back to safe ground, the side of a swimming bath in practice.

Wilson offered the drill to the Life Saving Society, and a handbook was produced by Wilson, with Sir Andrew Clark, and Dr W. Collingridge, the Medical Officer of Health for the Port of London co-operating. Sir Andrew was not altogether happy with some of the detail, but he was willing to reserve his judgement. The forms of resuscitation advised were:

the Marshall Hall method; considered the mildest;

the Silvester (not Sylvester as some writers have it) method; more vigorous, said to leave the patient with pains over the ribs, arms, neck and shoulders (but no doubt better than being drowned);

FASHIONS

'It is the fashion to drown. Why is it not the fashion to be able to swim? Will it be the fashion some day to know how to swim?'

Guts Muts, 1771

For recklessness in the face of danger the lady in this 1884 engraving takes some beating

Highgate Ponds where many of the early activities of the RLSS were held

the Howard method; practised in the United States, also inclined to leave pains.

Of these, the executive committee recommended the Silvester as the easiest to remember and having the advantage that the method could be carried out by just one operator.

The first year of the new society was devoted mainly to organisation, and William Wilson, in recognition of his services, was elected the first life governor of the society. There was great support for the Life Saving Society not only from the general public and the vast swimming fraternity but from industry; in particular Lever Brothers Ltd, the great soap manufacturers which had developed Port Sunlight, one of the first of the garden cities. Lever Brothers presented a valuable shield as a perpetual trophy as well as gold, silver and bronze medals for a new national competition, in which teams of four participated. In the first year of the competition twenty-four teams took part. The winning

THE BIGGIN SHIELD

Awards and honours may not be worldwide or even nationwide. One of the most interesting awards is the Biggin Shield, presented from 1905 by George H. Biggin for annual competition in rescue and resuscitation drills by teams from the elementary schools of Sheffield. It is one of the most treasured awards of the South Yorkshire branch of the RLSS UK. Quite recently the shield was damaged by intruders at the school where it was kept, and it was repaired by a silversmith who was trained by another silversmith who had been apprenticed to the man who had originally made the shield in 1905!

Mike Manley

The Marshall Hall method from a watercolour of 1862

A SLIGHT DISAGREEMENT

When the RLSS was formed, the rescue drill was devised by Mr Wilson of Glasgow. In due course the instructions were published. And they were wrong. On 8 September 1892 William Henry wrote to Mr Wilson:

The inaccuracies in the diagrams had previously been noticed by members of the society and we have had fresh ones prepared as the others are misleading to the teams.

But there seems to have been more to it than that. Later on in the letter Henry wrote:

We regret that you are dissatisfied with the methods which we have adopted in accomplishing the work which you as donor intended to be carried out.

What these dissatisfactions were we shall never know.

team took the Challenge Shield, the individual members receiving gold medals, the second team receiving silver medals, and the third and fourth teams bronze medals.

Of the thirty lifesaving cases reported in 1892, sixteen were directly due to members of the Life Saving Society or those who had been instructed by the society. One of the most publicised was the case of Edward Nicholls who had seen one of the many free demonstrations put on by the society. He rescued a lighterman who had fallen off his barge into thirty or forty feet of water at the Surrey Commercial Docks. Although the victim had been under water for three or four minutes, Nicholls used the knowledge he had acquired and restored the man to life.

Immediately after the handbook was published, many instruction classes were formed throughout the country, and participants took pleasure in taking proficiency examinations, and, if successful, winning proficiency medals. The requirements were to be able to swim, to have attended at least ten meetings for instruction, to be efficient in the drills including the ability to release oneself from the clutches of a desperate drowning person, and to be able to render resuscitation and treatment.

At the annual meeting of the Life Saving Society in 1893, the executive was able to announce that HRH the Duke of York (later King George V) had consented to become the president of the society. Since then, the Royal Family has always been deeply involved in what was to become the Royal Life Saving Society in 1904. HRH the Duke of York became vice-president, and Lord Ampthill, formerly Odo Russell, a member of the great Whig family and an ambassador to Germany, became acting president. There was no shortage of backing for the society, and soon great interest was being expressed abroad, especially in the Empire, where conditions were so different from those in Britain. In 1894 branches were formed in New South Wales and Manchester. The numbers of awards grew, and in 1894 334 medallions and certificates were awarded in the UK. In 1897 1,174 medallions and certificates were issued. The handbook was constantly being reissued.

Although branches were being formed throughout the British Empire, many of the countries had been involved in lifesaving for many years. As in Britain, swimmers had realised that their sport could be a means of preserving life. In Canada the Montreal Swimming Club had been formed in 1876, and the Dolphin Swimming Club of Toronto in 1881, and members of the Dolphin Swimming Club trained in lifesaving techniques, though the first organisation was probably the Harbour Life Saving Crew of Toronto, who manned boats to rescue the crews of cargo vessels in difficulty on Lake Ontario. The leading light in Canadian lifesaving was A. L. Cochrane, who had emigrated to Canada from Birmingham, England, and was the first overseas recipient of the Diploma.

This print dating from about 1880 illustrates the current bathing fashion. Although at that stage there was no organised lifesaving, the women in charge of the bathing huts could at least keep an eye on their charges

In Australia, the leading figure in the early years of lifesaving was John Ellis Stewart, a Devonian, who had arrived in Australia on the aptly named *True Briton* in 1869. He was heavily involved in the formation of the Victorian Humane Society in 1874, and as early as 1877 Australia had its own lifesaving manual and teaching lifesaving techniques in schools was much encouraged. The secretary of the Royal National Lifeboat Institute wrote from England congratulating Stewart on his work in education. Australia was 'in advance of the parent country in that respect.'

In 1897, the year of Queen Victoria's Jubilee — sixty years on the throne — throughout the country there were celebrations and events. This was the year when the first branch was started in Scotland. To honour the queen, the Life Saving Society organised an international gala at West India Dock in the presence of the Duke and Duchess of York, and representatives came from

Little has been written about changing social attitudes with regard to lifesaving. In the early days of the RLSS there would have been acute embarrassment in trying to rescue someone who may merely have been swimming and in no difficulties whatsoever

Belgium, Germany, Sweden, France, Australia and New Zealand. No doubt it was due to this that lifesaving was practised at the Auckland Swimming Club from 1898.

The Jubilee Gala was a wonderful opportunity for the society and it took full advantage of it. The first event was rescue and release drill, showing the methods of carrying a person in the water. These included the hold for a person being quiet and passive when being rescued, hold for a person violently struggling, and an easy method of carrying a person. Methods were also demonstrated of releasing oneself from the frenzied clutches of the drowning person.

Following these events demonstrations of resuscitation were carried out using the Silvester method. The instructions were now clear and free from ambiguity, as set out in the programme:

Turn the patient on his right side and clear the mouth, throat, and nostrils, to allow the air to enter the lungs. Pull the tongue forward and fasten it so that it does not fall back into the mouth and stop the air passages. Induce artificial respiration by means of the Silvester method. Endeavour to restore circulation and promote warmth by friction.

The teams that took part were fully catalogued:

Surrey Commercial Dock SC
Westminster LS Class
Webbe Institute
St Mathias' SC
London and India Docks SC
Goldsmiths' Institute SC
South-East Postal SC
St Mark's College School SC
Pacific SC
Coburg Road Board School
South African House SC
St Andrew's Home SC
Coventry Institute
West Ham School Teachers
Islington Vestry Officers' SC
Dreadnought SC
Camberwell LS Class
White Cross SC

A TREAT IN STORE

'I have been invited to inspect a variety of ladies' costumes as they encircle the fair forms of the opposite sex. Through other channels I have dwelt upon the bathing attire of ladies with commendable vigour and admiration, so I suppose there is a desire to show me something far prettier than has ever come under my personal observation. The proprietor of the bath assures me that I have a treat in store, a circumstance of which I was previously aware, and am prepared to demonstrate on the most undeniable testimony.'

The Swimmer Magazine, 1 March 1885

Some of these clubs put in more than one team. It is clear what a wide spectrum was covered, from schoolchildren to schoolteachers, from commercial organisations to local government.

The second event was the mile amateur championship, under the management of the Amateur Swimming Association, the winner of which would receive the Perpetual Challenge Cup for one year and a Gold Association Medal. A gold medal was also awarded to the second, and a silver medal to the third, and certificates were awarded to all those completing the distance in thirty-five minutes or under. The course was 220yd long, and there were eight lengths to the mile. Should the record be beaten the ASA would award a separate gold medal.

The English amateur record at the time was 26min 46.5sec

Highgate Bathers Scratch Race (Seniors) 1905

made by J. H. Tyers in 1896, the Australian amateur record was 27 min 45.4sec made by Percy Cavill in 1897, and the German amateur record (for 1500m) was 26min 2.5sec made by Arnold Toepfer in 1896. All these champions took part in the race, and there were twenty contestants all told. J. A. Jarvis of Leicester SC won in 32min 28.6sec. J. H. Tyers, the favourite, 'twice collided with swimmers but the impact was only trifling.'

The third event was a special 100yd scratch race, followed by a display of high and fancy diving by members of the Swedish Swimming Association, which had elevated diving or springing to an art form. 'Besides being good divers they are also fine floaters, their figures of an anchor, a star, and a circle, being particularly attractive.'

A FIRST

The first International Life Saving Congress was held in Marseilles in 1878.

This was followed by a 100yd rescue race, with competitors changing over halfway through, and the national graceful diving contest, the existing winner being H. S. Martin.

This test 'comprises at least one standing dive from heights not exceeding 3ft, 15ft, and 30ft. On entering the water each competitor must have his arms extended in advance of his head, the forefingers in contact, and the palms of the hands held downwards or together. The thighs and legs from the hips to the great toes, must be kept closed and the feet turned back until the instep is nearly in a straight line with the shin. No dive is counted, during which the competitor deviates from the above conditions or turns his back on entering the water.'

The diving was followed by a 100yd open amateur handicap race in four heats, with a total of 80 swimmers taking part, a 100yd open obstacle handicap race, a water polo match, and a final 100yd open handicap race, with eventually a dinner and the presentation of the prizes at the Holborn Restaurant. During the events a band played. Music at competitions and sports was customary, adding to the sense of occasion. The audience numbered 13,000.

The Championship Gala at the West India Docks was the first time the Life Saving Society had projected itself, and the details of the programme make interesting reading, as they established a pattern for all future events, especially in the mixture of instruc-

Heroic Rescue

1951: Robert Wardle, Alberta, Canada

Robert Wardle, a Boy Scout aged 16, of Alberta, Canada, rescued a two-year-old child from a water cistern. The entrance was only 18 inches square and entering this small hole he swam to the bottom — some ten feet. Lack of light, coldness of the water, refuse and debris hampered the rescuer but he was able to bring the child up through the manhole three feet from the surface of the water. The diameter of the cistern was only five feet which greatly limited movement by the rescuer. The victim had been in the water for ten minutes, breathing had stopped and she looked blue. Artificial respiration was applied by Robert and in due course the patient recovered but did not gain consciousness for four hours and was detained in hospital for two days.

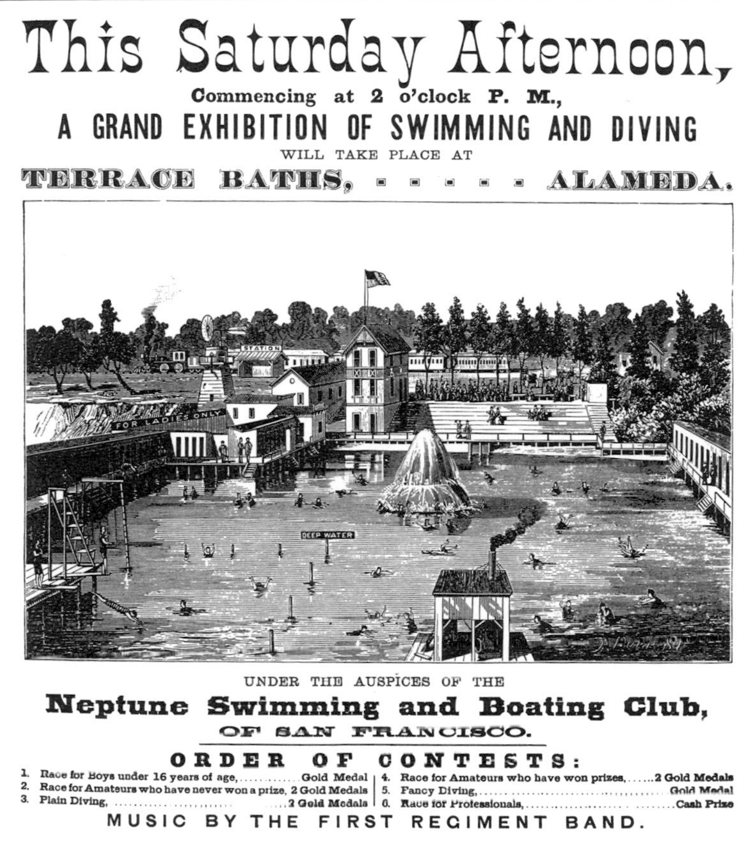

Lavish as swimming baths in the UK and on the Continent could be, especially in France, they did not match those in the US, which were even then well on the way to becoming water-leisure centres

tion, sport, and entertainment. Rescue-by-numbers was very suitable for public display, since synchronised movements were much easier to understand than mere actions as they gave a sense of style to the proceedings.

One distinction between the gala then and present-day competitions was that the Jubilee Gala was not sponsored, and on the last page of the programme there was an appeal for more public involvement in the society and, especially, 'substantial pecuniary support.' The Life Saving Society was not a rich concern; the surplus for 1897 was £9 8s 2d (£9.41). Another distinction was that in 1897 there were no women swimmers.

A consequence of the Jubilee Gala, and the presence of so many foreign swimmers, was an increase in interest in lifesaving abroad. Representatives of the Life Saving Society visited Sweden, resulting in the foundation of the Swedish Life Saving Society. The teaching of swimming in schools also made great headway, and instruction in lifesaving was given to the police. In 1900 an International Congress on Life Saving was held in connection with the Paris Exposition, and the secretary of the Life Saving Society attended, taking part in a lifesaving competition and being awarded the first prize — a gold medallion and a bronze statue valued at 1,000fr.

AMERICAN LIFESAVING

The first lifesaving society in the United States was the Massachusetts Humane Society formed in 1792

Many of the British competitions and events involving the Life Saving Society were held at Highgate Ponds, and when King Edward VII was crowned in 1902 a special display was given there with swimmers from the Colonies, the United States of America, France, Belgium, Sweden and the UK before 30,000 spectators. The trophy was awarded by the honorary president who, with the death of Queen Victoria, had now assumed the title of The Prince of Wales in place of the Duke of York. Edward VII became a patron of the society and presented a cup for competition. The British arm of the society being now thoroughly established, there was a good deal of enthusiasm for the creation of lifesaving societies abroad. There was a tour of Germany and Italy by a Life Saving Society team.

Classes were organised in India, and many continental societies asked for permission to translate the Life Saving Society handbook into their own languages. William Henry was particularly keen on establishing lifesaving societies throughout the world, and in subsequent years travelled widely.

King Edward VII was not merely a patron on paper, but actively involved himself in the work and activities of the Life Saving Society, visiting the Bath Club with Queen Alexandra and Princess Victoria to witness the first international competition for His Majesty's Cup, won by England with Hungary runner-up. It was only a matter of time before the king granted permission for the society to use the title 'Royal' and, although no Royal Charter

There are many methods of being taught to swim! A cartoon after the Punch *caricaturist Linley Sambourne*

Lord Desborough, one of the leading figures in the early days of the Royal Life Saving Society

was issued at the time, the Royal Life Saving Society came into being in 1904.

The number of UK awards increased year by year. By 1905 25,035 awards had been issued, and the annual galas at Highgate drew more and more spectators, although it was always difficult to compute how many; certainly the figures were in excess of 50,000. There was a major breakthrough in 1906 when the Lords of the Admiralty issued an order that instruction in swimming and lifesaving was to be given to all men in the Royal Navy for half an hour a day. All sailors were expected to swim 100yd, with clothes on (duck suits as a rule) but lifesaving was only to be taught to the more proficient. Classes for park-keepers were also held at various London public baths, and forty class meetings were given.

Lifesaving techniques had remained much the same, but in 1907 the whole system was reviewed. Although it had proved effective, the Silvester method was dropped in favour of the Schafer method; Sir Edward A. Sharpey-Schafer occupied the Chair of Physiology at Edinburgh University from 1889 until 1932 and had been a vice-president of the society for some years. The Schafer method was easy to understand and effective, easily

OLD FATHER THAMES

The River Thames has claimed many lives, both from accidents and from suicides. Typical of a Thames rescue was that carried out on 14 July 1885 when at 2.45 in the morning PC John Jenkins saw a man mount the parapet of Waterloo Bridge and throw himself into the river. Without hesitation, Jenkins unfastened his belt and jumped after him, and although the attempted suicide struggled, having no wish to be saved, the constable seized him and held onto him until both of them were picked up a considerable distance downstream by a police boat. The danger to the policeman was considerable. The distance jumped was forty-three feet, the river was running at six miles an hour and there was a thick mist.

Unquestionably one of the reasons why the RLSS thrived and is thriving is because of the quality of the members. The photograph is of the 'Highgate Lifebuoy' W. S. McKenzie, known as 'Grandpa', aged 84 and still active

carried out by even the half-experienced and learner.

'Lay the subject face downwards on the ground, then without stopping to remove the clothing the operator should at once place himself in position astride or at one side of the subject, facing his head and kneeling upon one or both knees. He then places his hands flat over the lower part of the back (on the lowest ribs), one on each side, and then gradually throws the weight of his body forward on to them so as to produce firm pressure, which must not be violent, upon the patient's chest. By this means the air, and water if any, are driven out of the patient's lungs. Immediately thereafter the operator raises his body slowly so as to remove the pressure, but the hands are left in position. This forward and backward movement is repeated every four or five seconds; in other words, the body of the operator is swayed slowly forwards and backwards upon the arms from twelve to fifteen times a minute, and should be continued for at least half an hour, or until the natural respirations are resumed.'

It is much to the credit of the Royal Life Saving Society that it could be pragmatic, and that it did not put convenience first. It needed a good deal of courage to drop the Silvester method when it had been taught to tens of thousands of people, and of course it meant that the handbooks, published in huge quantities, would need to be revised to take in the new system. Not everyone liked the change; the Royal Humane Society advocated the Silvester method and the National Lifeboat Institution preferred Marshall Hall's technique. However in the United States the Red Cross, after a good deal of cogitation, voted in favour of the Schafer method.

In all organisations of a voluntary nature, there is great interest in winning awards and medallions, and it provides a spur. In 1908 the Award of Merit was instituted to encourage swimming and lifesaving when fully attired. It was classed between the Bronze Medallion and the Diploma, the highest award, instituted in 1896. The only danger of awards is that there can be so many classes and sub-classes that they become meaningless bits of metal. Fortunately the Royal Life Saving Society has never fallen into this trap, and all their awards have kept their prestige and have never been issued as a matter of course.

Throughout this exciting period in the expansion of the RLSS more and more branches were being formed. In 1908 the Ulster branch came into being, and in Canada the Ontario branch was formed in 1908, Quebec in 1909, Manitoba in 1910, and British Columbia in 1912. William Henry visited many of the British Empire countries; Canada in 1909, and Australia and New Zealand in 1910, where he handed out photographs of himself and was reported as saying that sharks 'did not bite vegetarians.' The first New Zealand branch was formed in Wanganui.

There would soon be a presence in all the main English-speaking countries of the Empire.

SEAMAN'S FRIEND

What was the seaman's friend? This was an invention by W. H. Mallison in 1804. We know it better as a lifebelt, and Mallison wanted to introduce it into the Royal Navy as an aid to swimming. The Royal Navy was not at all keen. The seaman's friend took up too much room, and besides, it did not want its sailors to swim in case they deserted!

1911–43 *Diving Deeper*

When Edward VII died, King George V consented to become patron. As the Duke of York twenty years earlier he had been intimately involved in the early days of the Royal Life Saving Society. Lord Desborough became president in 1910, having been acting president since 1901. He remained president until his death at a great age in 1944. Lord Desborough was extremely active, and as he was chairman of the Thames Conservancy, he arranged for an instruction tour down the Thames to educate lock-keepers, weir-keepers and ferrymen in lifesaving, an important project, for the Thames was increasingly used in leisure pursuits.

Lord Desborough was a sportsman in his own right. Born in 1855, he was educated at Harrow and Balliol College, Oxford, playing cricket for Harrow, representing Oxford in the three-mile race against Cambridge, and participated in the Boat Races of 1877-8. And that was only the beginning of his sporting career. He climbed in the Alps, shot in the Rocky Mountains, swam twice across Niagara, stroked an eight across the English Channel, and was a champion fencer at the age of fifty. He also won the punting championship three years running. As sportsmen were at the heart of the Royal Life Saving Society, he was the ideal person to have at the helm, even though he also had a distinguished political career as well and was an MP between 1900 and 1905 for the Wycombe Division of Buckinghamshire, the location of Taplow Court, the family home.

The King Edward VII cup with the winners' clubs engraved. Readers with good eyesight will note that HMS Ganges *did very well*

He was also active in establishing the RLSS abroad and when visiting Canada in 1911 he was partly responsible for the formation of a branch in British Columbia, presenting it with a silver-gilt challenge cup for competition amongst its members. Another silver-gilt cup was awarded for competitions in swimming and lifesaving in the Boy Scouts.

William Henry was also continuing to travel the Empire, encouraging the new branches and urging the formation of fresh

The headstone of William Henry in Highgate Cemetery. He died 20 March 1928, arter nearly forty years devoted to the cause of lifesaving

ones. In 1911 he toured South Africa and the South African and Southern Rhodesian branches were the direct result. In many of his trips abroad he was involved in the controversies of the day and spoke on the 'vexed question of mixed bathing' when he visited New Zealand in 1910.

Unquestionably the Royal Life Saving Society had thrived because of the quality of the members. It must always be remembered that the active members, even many of the administrative members, were swimmers, and British sportsmen of the time enjoyed a good deal of prestige and had confidence, as they expected to win. It is no wonder that they were determined that their society would succeed.

The Edwardian period has often been called the golden age of sport. As John Arlott so rightly said, even in 1890 any observer must have noted a steady building up, everywhere in Britain, towards a standard of sporting performance and participation never known before in the world. Sport was accepted as part of the domestic setting and, except in boxing and some kinds of athletics where America was superior, no other country had been developing sports long enough or thoroughly enough to provide serious competition to the best of the British. Every sport had its specialist magazines, sometimes more than one — and that included swimming — and were widely supported, although there was still an uneasy line between amateurs and professionals.

Swimming was a mass spectator sport, especially when competitions included diving, races, and what might be termed entertainments. It was easy to include lifesaving demonstrations in the programmes as part of a very acceptable package. Swimming had been given an additional boost by the successes in the Olympic Games of 1908 where the British swimming contestants came away with four gold medals (the British took fifty-six golds in all!).

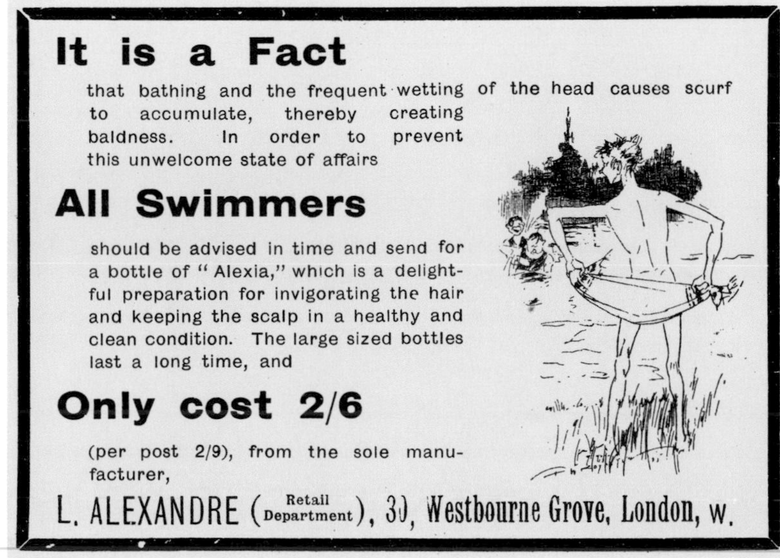

Although this advertisement dates from 1895, there have never been any shortages of attempts to capitalise on the real or imaginary perils of swimming, though whether it is a fact that 'bathing and the frequent wetting of the head causes scurf to accumulate, thereby creating baldness' was, and is, open to question

The provision of danger signs became ever more important as water sports became ever more popular

With the coming of World War I the golden age went for good. As many of the active members of the society were young and belonged to the class of person never backward in coming forward when the needs of the country demanded, many thousands were killed in the war. The decimation of a whole section of society in the trenches of the Western Front has thrown a shadow over history. But with the coming of peace, the RLSS resumed its task, that of saving life.

The following years were of consolidation and review, revaluating rescue and resuscitation techniques, considering new innovations and inventions that would make lifesavers even more efficient. New branches were constantly being opened and expanded. Alberta, Canada, dates from 1924, and in 1932 a branch opened in Victoria on Canada's Vancouver Island.

New manual resuscitation techniques were constantly being evolved, the most significant being the Holger Nielsen method developed in 1931 and eventually adopted by the RLSS as well as by the St John Ambulance Association.

On 20 March 1928 William Henry died, and Lord Desborough presented the William Henry Memorial Cup to the RLSS as a perpetual memorial to the man who had founded the RLSS and who, up to his death, had never ceased in his efforts to promote the society at home and abroad. The cup was to be awarded to branches that achieved the best results in lifesaving. Marks to the branches were awarded on a set scale:

for each Elementary certificate gained	1 point
for each Proficiency Certificate gained	3 points
for each Hon Instructor's Certificate gained	7 points
for each Award of merit gained	12 points
for each Diploma awarded	25 points

ICE-BOUND

Frozen water is always a temptation to skaters. And sometimes a frozen river is a tempting short cut; often it is equivalent to crossing a busy railway line on foot. In 1887 a young girl attempted to cross the ice-bound River Soar at Leicester when the ice broke and she became immersed in fourteen feet of water. A man went part of the way across the ice to try and rescue her, but realising the foolhardiness of the attempt he returned. A boy of seventeen, Albert Battison, went out and dived through the hole in the ice and managed to get hold of the girl. In coming up he had to break the ice with his head. If he had failed to do this there is no question that he would have drowned. Battison was awarded the Stanhope Gold Medal of the Royal Humane Society.

SHOPPING LIST

'Materials employed in the various processes for recovering suspended animations from drowning, viz:

Small bottle of rectified spirit of wine
Small bottle of white wine vinegar
Small bottle of sweet oil
Small bottle of white French brandy
Small bottle of volatile *sal ammoniac*
Small bottle of vitriolic aether
Small bottle of mustard seed
A machine for injecting the smoke of tobacco
A leather tube, together with a pair of bellows, for inflating the lungs
Another tube of leather, for introducing the medicines into the stomach
A small syringe for clearing the throat of mucus
Three woollen covers or blankets
Four brushes and six woollen cloths for performing friction
Several emetics
Two lancets for blood letting
One pound of tobacco
A roller and a cushion for use in venesection
Two quills, a sponge, and some lint
A pocket knife
An apparatus for striking fire
Camomile and elder flowers
Common salt
Printed copy of rules and directions for treating the drowned'

The British Herbal and Family Physician (1653)
by Nicholas Culpeper
— copy dated on fly leaf 1872

William Henry's wife presented a cup to the RLSS, known as the Mrs Henry Cup, open to ladies' colleges, schools and other educational establishments. The central executive of the RLSS appealed for donations to the William Henry Memorial Fund to recognise his great humanitarian work, and the first charge on the fund was a stone to mark Henry's grave in Highgate Cemetery. In the centenary year of the RLSS there are plans to clean and restore this monument to the founder.

The rest of the money was to provide a replica of the cup for the winning branches of the William Henry Memorial Cup as a permanent trophy. There were now several trophies competed for on an annual basis:

The King's Cup
The William Henry Memorial Cup
The Darnell Excellence Trophy, open to all affiliated public schools and colleges
The General Excellence Trophy, open to mercantile training schools, naval schools, and military schools for boys
The Ladies' Silver Cup, for competition among ladies' clubs or sections of clubs
The Affiliated Clubs Challenge Shield
The Mrs Henry Cup

★ COME & SEE
THE FILMING
of
THE LIFE-SAVING DEMONSTRATION IN THE THAMES
by
LADY MARY ALINGTON
at
POULSEN'S CLUB
DATCHET
SATURDAY NEXT
JULY 18
STARTING at 3.30 p.m.

Not only was there a film to see promoting the RLSS, but a film of the film!

The Dover Lifeguards 1932 made up of police officers. They are proudly lining up to receive the gift of a reel and line from the Daily Sketch. *Those were the days when tabloids had their hearts in the right place*

In 1930 71,563 awards were issued. Branches were formed in Liverpool and Northumberland and Durham. In the subsequent years Leeds, South Wales, North and East Yorkshire, and Birmingham were all to have their own branches, most of which exist to this day.

In the British Empire, the work of the RLSS was constantly in the public eye. Conditions were often completely different to those in the UK, and in 1932 the new Zealand Surf Life Saving Association was formed with the blessings of the local RLSS branch to cater for activities that were totally unknown in Britain. One of the main differences between the British and the Commonwealth branches was that in the larger Commonwealth countries the branches were autonomous, and insistent on keeping it that way.

To publicise its work the RLSS in Britain produced a lifesaving film, keeping up to date by using all the sophisticated promotional means available to it. The main aim of the film was to assist instructors throughout the Empire. Visual aids have often proved to be more easily assimilated than written material, especially for those whose first language may not be that in which the handbook was written — English. One of the main participants in the film, Lady Alington, later gave a talk on the radio on lifesaving, resulting in a great many enquiries from those who had not previously had any dealings whith the RLSS.

The Diploma had continued to be the highest honour granted by the society, and a gold medal was now given to all successful Diploma candidates who had obtained 80 per cent marks for each section of the practical and theoretical part.

In 1932 the numbers of awards dropped slightly. This was attributed to the greater stringency of the examinations, but it was only a temporary hiccup. A major event of the year was the inauguration of the Lifeguard Corps*, which might be described as the infantry of the RLSS. All holders of the Bronze Medallion

THE DUCK PUDDLE

Open-air swimming pools have their attendants, but not often do they have a full-time caretaker. Even less often is a cottage built just for the caretaker. This happened at the 'duck puddle' in 1851. This was the name given to the swimming pool of Harrow school. In 1826 it was full of frogs, water-rats and, it was believed, eels. The schoolboys preferred to swim in the nearby canal. You won't find the 'duck puddle' today, for the pool was rebuilt in 1881, 500ft long and an average of 60ft wide. It had a system of lock gates to allow the pool to be emptied, cleaned, and refilled without stopping the bathing. There was also an iron bridge across it spanning 43ft.

*Later to be designated the RLSS Lifeguards

What could look more innocent? A placid stretch of water, houses nearby . . .

The 1930s was the age of the pool in the garden, and often familiarity bred contempt, especially for the young

were invited to join. A conference was held with the St John Ambulance Association so that uniformity of practice could be organised and it was agreed that the St John Ambulance Association should use the Schafer method of resuscitation as carried out by the RLSS, though St John went over to the Holger Nielsen method in 1952 (the method disappeared from the instructions of the RLSS in 1966).

Throughout their parallel histories there was always help and friendly feelings between the two voluntary organisations and in the earliest days when the Life Saving Society (as it was then) was striving for credibility, the organ of St John *First Aid* always had an enthusiastic section devoted to the work and progress of the Life Saving Society.

Of great importance to the future of the RLSS abroad was the Empire Conference held on 28-9 July 1933, with representatives from Australia, New Zealand, South Africa, India and Great Britain. One of the issues discussed was the importance of a uniform standard of efficiency in the gaining of the society's awards.

In 1934 the Resuscitation Certificate was instituted, with examinations twice a year. The fee was two shillings (10p). The test

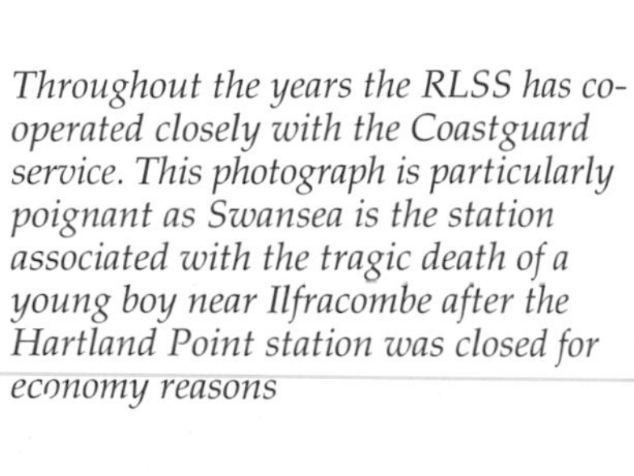

Throughout the years the RLSS has co-operated closely with the Coastguard service. This photograph is particularly poignant as Swansea is the station associated with the tragic death of a young boy near Ilfracombe after the Hartland Point station was closed for economy reasons

was in two sections:

drill for the Schafer method of at least five minutes, and promotion of circulation;

a viva voce test comprising questions on resuscitation in case of drowning, in case of suffocation from smoke, gas, fumes, etc, and in case of electric shock.

It is clear that the RLSS was widening its curriculum.

And it was receiving more newspaper coverage. The *Daily Sketch*

From the early days it was necessary to drive home to youngsters that a non-contact rescue was in every way better, whether it was using line, as here, towing or buoyancy aids

A TOP RESCUER

One of the great lifesavers of all time was Mark Addy, born in Manchester in 1838. His father was a boat-builder and waterman, and Addy gained his knowledge of swimming at Greengate Baths, Salford. He was only thirteen when he saved a boy, who was in danger of drowning in the River Irwell, by means of a hastily constructed raft. After he had rescued thirty-seven people from drowning he was honoured by the city, and awarded a purse of 200 guineas (£210). He went on to rescue more than fifty people, but his end was hastened by a rescue he effected in the River Irwell where 'sewer and other noxious gases make the water exceeding filthy.' He did not regret it. On his death-bed in 1890 he said:

'Yes, it is true I have saved many lives, but the best work I ever did was saving that little lad on Whit Monday. I think more about that than all the rest. To see the joy of his brother and sister when I brought him out, to feel their grip round my legs, and hear them thank me a hundred times, was more to me than all else besides; it was better than the big meeting, and the purse of gold given at the town hall.'

backed demonstrations of lifesaving drill at seaside places. The Lifeguard Corps was something that the man in the street could associate with, and their presence at danger spots was recognised and appreciated.

Many of the founder members of the Life Saving Society were falling away and 1935 saw not only the death of the first patron of the society, King George V, but Sydney J. Monks, who had been associated with William Henry since 1898. Like Henry, Monks was a celebrated swimmer, and had won many competitions. After being William Henry's right-hand man in the many demonstrations of lifesaving that Henry had given he had taken over the job of chief secretary when Henry died.

As with all monarchs, including Edward VIII later Duke of Windsor, King George VI became patron of the RLSS and a great fillip was given to the society when Princess Elizabeth and Princess Margaret were given lessons in swimming and lifesaving.

Membership of the Lifeguard Corps was now up to 11,000, and 54 rescues had been effected during 1936 (46 rescues during 1935). A cadet branch of the Lifeguard Corps was formed for boys between fourteen and eighteen. In 1937 a target of 100,000 awards was proposed, with the slogan 'Every Swimmer a Lifesaver.' It was not quite reached, but it was the following year with 105,710 awards, a magnificent achievement.

However, so far as the general public was concerned, the most newsworthy event of 1937 was the passing of the Elementary Certificate by Princess Elizabeth. This was widely publicised in the press and, as Princess Elizabeth had a wide following amongst children (along with Shirley Temple!), many young people sought to emulate her. The following year Princess Elizabeth gained the Intermediate Certificate (and Princess Margaret the Elementary Certificate), resulting in more newspaper coverage.

The great popular appeal of the RLSS at this time coincided with a drive by the government for a 'fitter Britain', and there was great enthusiasm for all kinds of exhibitions and demonstrations organised by the National Fitness Council. So far as the RLSS was concerned, the crowning event was a demonstration in the Lord Mayor's Show on 9 November 1938, seen by thousands of Londoners lining the route and millions on the newsreels in the country's cinemas. The cinema was the most powerful medium of its day.

With the coming of World War II in September 1939, the RLSS became, along with the St John Ambulance Association, the ARP (Air Raids Precautions), the WVS (Women's Voluntary Service), an active and valuable arm of civil defence. The accent was now not on rescue from water but on resuscitation. The new handbook *Artificial Respiration — Are You Prepared?* emphasised this. There was a special examination to train and form a Respiration Service Corps, and 120,000 free copies of a pamphlet giving instruction in the Schafer method were distributed nationwide.

Lectures and demonstrations were arranged throughout the country, and in 1941 instruction was extended to children over fourteen years old, and a Junior Respiration Examination was introduced, the first person to pass it being Princess Elizabeth. Wartime conditions cut down on the customary work of the RLSS, but even in 1941 there were 90,009 awards. The society, as did many others, worked under great disadvantages and stress. Little paper was available for the necessary work involved in running a great organisation, and the shortage of metal meant that Bronze Medallions and other awards were replaced by certificates, to be replaced by the appropriate medal when conditions changed.

One disadvantage was that the nation's swimming pools had been given over to other purposes, and those that were still used for swimming purposes, situated mainly in the large towns and cities, were often subject to bomb damage. The examiners and teachers, as with most other volunteer workers, were also often deeply involved with civil defence, and as the war continued more and more of them joined the armed forces.

Sometimes it seemed as if the war would go on for ever, but eventually the tide turned, and it was time to think of the future, of a world at peace.

A polite enquiry! Nearly being drowned was still, surprisingly, regarded as humorous

Polite Rescuer. "EXCUSE MY GLOVE."

1943 – 72

The Commonwealth Dimension

THE MOUNTBATTEN PERIOD

In 1943 Admiral Lord Louis Mountbatten became vice-president, despite all the calls on his time; early in the year he had attended the Casablanca Conference to join with the British Chiefs of Staff in a deep discussion of strategy in the Mediterranean, and it was Mountbatten who stressed that an invasion of Europe in 1943 was impossible. After the Casablanca Conference he returned to London to begin planning Operation Husky, the invasion of Sicily. This was Mountbatten's own idea, as the original plan had been to invade Sardinia, a dangerous project as Sardinia was beyond the range of Allied fighter cover.

Lord Mountbatten was to become a stalwart of the RLSS and a key figure in its expansion in the Empire, soon to be the Commonwealth, and his importance in the organisation can hardly be overemphasised. Eventually, well into the future, he was commemorated for all time in the name given to the new headquarters of the RLSS in Studley, Warwickshire, Mountbatten House.

The RLSS continued its war work along with its traditional tasks, and the Unigrip method of rescue was demonstrated to diplomats, officers of the armed forces and other prominent

Heroic Rescue

1956: Bernard Litwack, of Southport, Lancashire

On the morning of a cold day in April, Bernard Litwack saw a man trapped on a sandbank on a rapidly rising tide. He immediately undressed and swam three-quarters of a mile against a strong tide. After thirty-five minutes he arrived at the sandbank, still not entirely covered. A policeman saw the situation from the seafront and arranged for a rescue boat. When the boat arrived at the sandbank the two men were up to their chests in water. Litwack had been an hour in the water. He was in an exhausted state, and was detained for some hours at the hospital where he was given oxygen.

people at Marshall Street baths. A little-publicised aspect of the work of the RLSS was the provision of books of instruction and information for Allied prisoners of war. Practice in rescue and resuscitation was both mentally and physically stimulating, and no doubt many of the prisoners of war who passed examinations whilst they were interned joined the RLSS when they were demobilised.

The number of lifeguards was increasing year by hear

In 1944 another bastion of the RLSS died, Lord Desborough, and Princess Elizabeth consented to become the society's vice-patron. At this time, despite flying bombs and rockets, the head-quarters were moved from New Malden to 14 Devonshire Street, Portland Place, London W1. Lord Mountbatten took over the

One of the sad features of the postwar scene is the reduction in the numbers of traditional swimming baths such as this

Lord Mountbatten making a presentation

presidency at the express wish of King George VI, but his duties overseas, especially his appointment in 1946 as Viceroy of India, prevented him from taking a major role in the RLSS at first and E. H. Oxlade, the senior vice-president, acted on his behalf. Lord Mountbatten was one of only five men to become a Supreme Allied Commander during the war. The others were Generals Eisenhower, MacArthur, Wilson, and Field Marshal Alexander, and it is something of a coincidence that when Alexander became Governor-General of Canada he became honorary patron of the Canadian branch of the RLSS, having been a vice-president of the society in England.

With peace, the RLSS once more returned to its traditional duties. In 1947 a vicious outbreak of poliomyelitis (infantile paralysis) caused the closing of public baths, and children were stopped from all involvement in swimming and lifesaving instruction. Nevertheless, there was no let up in the work load of the society and the new medium of television was utilised to demonstrate its duties. The venue was the Marshall Street baths, and the

GOOD FOR HIM!

'J. B. Johnson, contrary to expectation, will this season resume his exploits from the head of Blackpool Pier. I hear he is a total abstainer, and intends to observe a long course of sobriety.'

The Swimmer Magazine,
23 Feb 1884

Heroic Rescue

1957: Peter Critchley, of Cheadle, Cheshire

On an afternoon in March a boy of seven wearing Wellington boots slipped from a concrete jetty at Bangor, North Wales, and was swept out to sea on a strong tide. A man went to his rescue, but was grasped round the throat by the boy and both were soon in difficulties. Critchley, who had recently undergone an operation to his left arm, dived in and swam thirty yards against a strong ebb tide. By the time he reached them the man was unconscious and the boy semi-conscious. Critchley brought them both to shore, where they were given artificial respiration.

commentator was the chief secretary of the society, Capt A. E. Biscoe, who was awarded the OBE in recognition of the work of the society. Another long-serving member of the RLSS died, John V. Hudson, who had been honorary treasurer since 1926, and to serve as a memorial the John V. Hudson Memorial Trophy was introduced, presented annually to the school, club or association (except police training centres) that won the most bronze crosses and bars in the year.

A new competition was instituted, the Beatrice Staynes Life Saving Competition for the Lifeguard Corps. Miss Beatrice Staynes had been representative for Leicester. The number of lifeguards was generally increasing year by year — 1,300 new members including cadets in 1948, 1,894 in 1949, 1,453 in 1950. Awards were now at the level of 1938. The Mountbatten Medal for Saving Life from Drowning was introduced, to be presented each year to the best rescue of the year, unless such a rescue had been honoured in some other way. The first recipient of the medal was a Canadian, Robert Wardle of Alberta; the second was a fifteen-year-old girl, Sally Jupp, from Enfield.

HRH the Princess Elizabeth attended the Diamond Jubilee Council Meeting in 1951 and unveiled the Mountbatten Medal Panel, and with the death of King George VI Queen Elizabeth II

The Beatrice Staynes Lifeguard Corps Trophy

THANKS VERY MUCH!

'E. J. Reddish, who is so popular at Llandudno as a swimming instructor, has been starring in the Lancashire district. Last week he appeared in his tank at the Gaiety Theatre, Oldham, before a crowded house, and his performance received flattering approval.'

The Swimmer Magazine, 23 Feb 1884

took over as patron. It was reported that the total number of awards issued since the inception of the RLSS was approaching three million.

In 1955 it was resolved to reorganise the RLSS. In its new form the society would comprise five self-governing national branches in Australia, New Zealand, South Africa, Canada and the United Kingdom. The title of each branch would be the Royal Life Saving Society followed by the name of the country. The whole would be co-ordinated by a Commonwealth Council. Many of the branches had built up an infrastructure of their own. In 1948 the Canadian Council of Branches had been formed.

Canada was fortunate in that the University of Toronto had granted the National and Ontario branches office accommodation, and 'this most acceptable contribution has made it possible for the Canadian society to use its limited finances in promoting the technical and educational aspects of our work.'

To further the implementation of the RLSS in its new form, a petition would be submitted to HM The Queen for the grant of a Supplemental Charter, and to assist in the change-over a Shadow Commonwealth Council was to be set up immediately. It was proposed that the presidents of councils of the five Commonwealth countries should become vice-presidents of the RLSS. Not everyone was happy with the new situation, and this was referred to by the president, Lord Mountbatten, who had done much to promote the reorganisation, at the annual council meeting in May 1958:

> 'I would like to say a word about the principle underlying our plans, because there have been times when I have thought that some of the support which has been given to them has been lip-service or half-hearted rather than the genuine whole-hearted support which they must have throughout the Society

Heroic Rescue

1958: Duncan McLean Campbell of Fulham, London

In September 1958 two children bathing at Withnoe Beach, Whitsands Bay, north Cornwall, got into difficulties, and were being dragged out to sea in a strong south-westerly wind and a heavy surf. The alarm was raised when the children were about a hundred yards out and Campbell swam to the rescue. The first to be rescued was an eleven-year-old boy, who panicked, and seized Campbell round the neck. Campbell was obliged to restrain him but, by telling the boy to hold his breath when a wave was about to hit them the boy gained confidence. As a consequence of his instructions Campbell himself swallowed a good deal of water. When forty yards from shore, Campbell handed the boy over to a helper with belt and lifeline. The other child in the water was a girl, fifty yards out and swimming parallel with the beach. Although exhausted, Campbell went out again, and persuaded the girl to swim alongside him to the beach. This she did, until she was fifteen yards out, where she collapsed. Campbell carried her to the shore. Another man who had entered the water to effect a rescue drowned. It was only with the greatest difficulty that Campbell was prevented from going back and trying to find him.

The Mountbatten Medal awarded once a year for an act of great heroism

Rather a saucy comment on Working Parties in general!

WORKING PARTY

Z Z

RLSS

Z

Z

WILL YOU KINDLY STOP PREVENTING ACCIDENTS UNTIL WE HAVE DECIDED IF THEY ARE DANGEROUS!

if they are to be brought to a workable conclusion. Our scheme, as you know, is a novel one and not entirely easy to achieve but it is worth while and it can be a success if it is given the goodwill and support which it deserves.'

Lord Mountbatten was never a person to mince words.

'There is no room in it for parochialism and selfish narrow-minded thinking.'

And there was a reminder of what such attitudes could lead to:

'the disappearance of the Royal Life Saving Society as we know it today.'

Lord Mountbatten then referred to the first Shadow Commonwealth Council which had been attended by the High Commissioners for Canada and Australia and the Deputy High Commissioner for the Union of South Africa, and where it had been suggested that an approach should be made to the governments of the members of the council to obtain annual grants.

It is interesting to compare the lifesaving awards and awards for artificial respiration for this very important and historic year, 1958:

UK	98,375
Canada	15,198
Australia	46,895
New Zealand	16,887
South Africa	4,171

Today the position is very different, with most awards being won by Canada, with Australia in second place, and the UK third, concrete evidence of the enormous expansion of Commonwealth lifesaving.

In addition there were 3,261 awards gained by units of the society from non-branch areas overseas including Trinidad, Barbados, Hong Kong, Ceylon, Jamaica, India, Singapore, Kuala

Heroic Rescue

1959: Police Constable Richard Cooke of Nottingham City Police

PC Cooke with his two small children and another member of the family was watching a motor cruiser as it attempted to negotiate a lock on the River Soar. The owner of the cruiser went to open the lock gates, leaving his wife on the bank holding stern and bow lines. There was a surge of water, and the wife released the lines, shouting to her husband. He ran back to her and in the confusion they both fell in. Neither could swim. PC Cooke dived in fully-clothed except for his jacket, swam a hundred yards diagonally to their rescue through turbulent waters, towing the man to another motor cruiser which had arrived on the scene. The wife was floating face downwards under the surface of the water, but Cooke rescued her as well, and applied artificial respiration successfully. The action was even more meritorious because Cooke had recently left hospital after recovering from a serious illness.

Heroic Rescue

1960: David Taylor of Preston, Lancashire

On the night of 28 November 1960. David Taylor, a seventeen-year-old apprentice electrician heard cries for help from the River Gribble. It was pitch dark. Without hesitation he dived in at a place where the river is 120ft wide. He found a woman who was a non-swimmer and who struggled violently as he tried to rescue her. After being carried fifty yards downriver he managed to get her to the bank, six feet high, where he was assisted by a passerby. Taylor then gave the woman artificial respiration until the arrival of an ambulance.

Presentation of the 1960 Mountbatten Medal to David Taylor by HM Queen Elizabeth the Queen Mother

Lumpur, Penang, Pakistan, and Nairobi.

The sixty-eighth Annual General Meeting of the council of the society was held on 30 May 1959. Lord Mountbatten presided, declaring:

> 'There can be no doubt that since its foundation in 1891 our society has done a magnificent job for humanity, but its growth as a Commonwealth-wide body has made its present organisation completely out of date. While change is often a matter for regret, I believe there will be few, if any, members who will not welcome the changes which we are now about to make, and which will enable our society to go forward to even greater success in the future than it has had in the past.'

Towards the end of the meeting Lord Mountbatten asked the national president of the UK, Sir Cecil Wakeley, to accept, on behalf of the society, a presentation bell supported between two dolphins and surmounted by a Tudor crown. The wording on the base reads:

> 'To the Royal Life Saving Society from the first Grand President to commemorate the granting of the new Commonwealth Charter 1959.'

Closing the meeting Lord Mountbatten said:

'This concludes the most historic meeting since the original meeting founding the society. I believe that the reason why the governments have given us grants is because the prime ministers in each case appreciate that societies like ours, which have

A QUESTION OF DEPORTMENT

'I beg to suggest an addition to the meagre costumes worn by swimmers at entertainments to which ladies are invited. Alsò, it would be as well if young men would remember that they are in the presence of ladies, and that therefore great cautiousness should be exercised as regards their deportment. It is almost needless to observe that at no time is it interesting to observe the completion of a swimmer's toilet; but when that individual elects to postpone his last efforts until well in front of the spectators, the contortions exhibited are anything but graceful, and detract from the beauty of the natationist.'

The Swimmer Magazine, 23 Feb 1884.

a voluntary association between the various parts of the Commonwealth, form some of the strongest ties that keep the Commonwealth together. It is far more important than just an act of lifesaving, it is the common purpose, the common title, and now the common overall organisation of the Commonwealth Council. So I think today we have written a page in Commonwealth history and all of us who have been associated with it can feel very proud.'

THE NAKED TRUTH

'Would proprietors of baths compel their patrons to wear drawers during the forthcoming season? I am not over-particular, but I think the practice should extend to boys, particularly precocious ones.'

The Swimmer Magazine, 1 Mar 1884

A Supplemental Charter was granted to the RLSS by HM the Queen on 27 January 1960, on which date the new organisation came officially into force.

The new form of the RLSS created much enthusiasm throughout the Commonwealth, and new clubs were formed. Some branches had been in existence for many years, some were new. Although lifesaving had been carried out in Malaysia since 1927, and members of the Penang Chinese Swimming Club had been Bronze Medallion holders, Malaysia had its own branch in 1964, and would shortly be issuing 5,000 awards a year of its own.

Mombasa scored a first when eight adults, the first to be trained, took their examinations and looked forward to obtaining a Distinction Award and a Diploma. This was thought to be over-ambitious at that stage. On the other hand the Malta branch of the society had been founded in 1926. In Malta's earlier days the

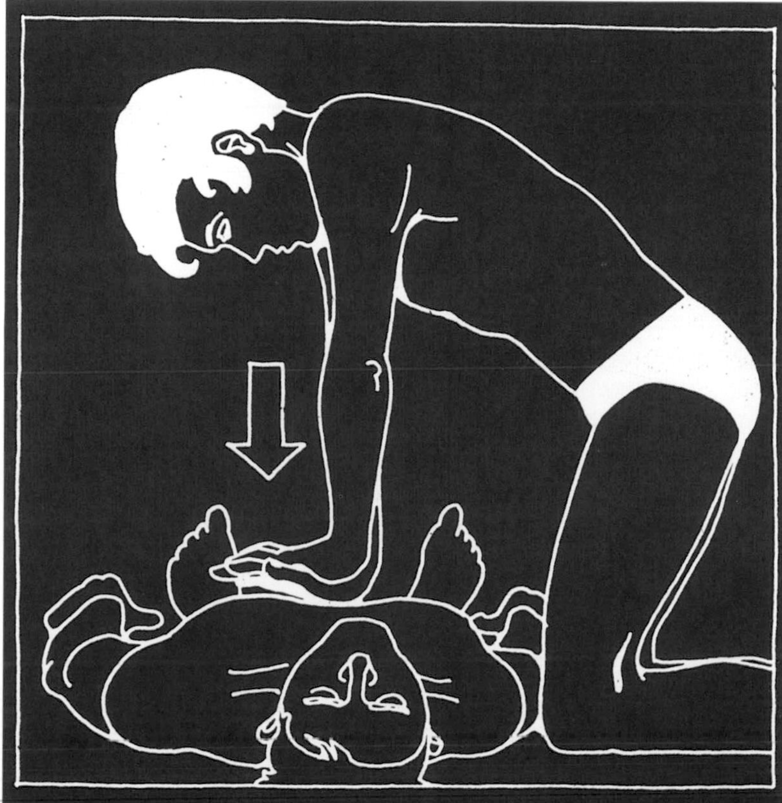

Cardiac compression—one operator

During the period prior to the acceptance on aesthetic grounds of mouth to mouth or mouth to nose resuscitation (Expired Air Resuscitation) cardiac compression was one of the key weapons in the lifesaver's armoury. And the introduction of EAR has by no means made the older methods obsolete

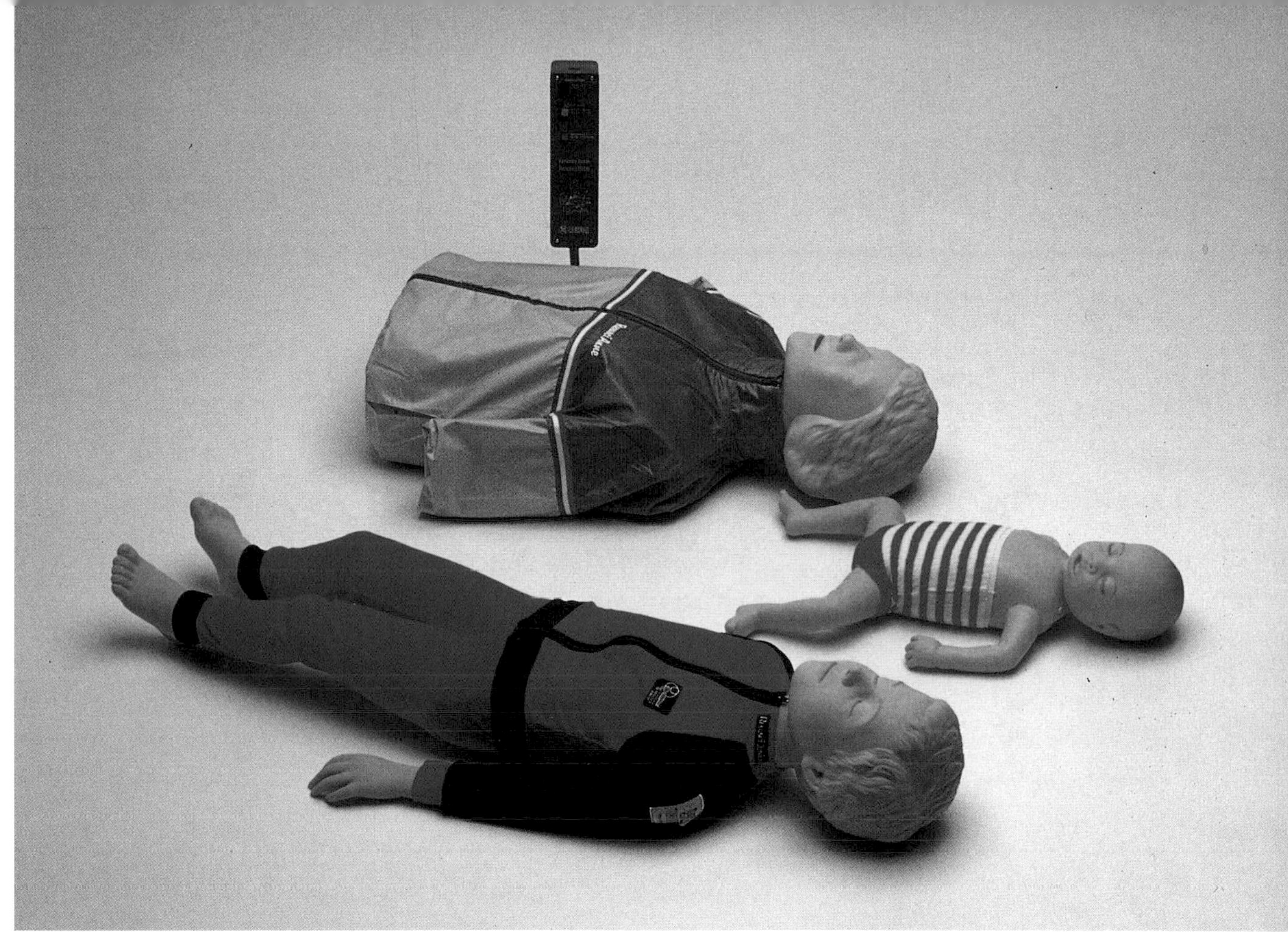

Objections to mouth to mouth resuscitation were partly overcome by the introduction of manikins for the students to practise on

armed services had been the most enthusiastic, but with the prospect of an independent Malta and the departure of the British forces the organisers were anxious that the civilian population should be involved. The situation was also difficult because there were no swimming pools on the island.

In Hong Kong, 1,436 awards for proficiency in lifesaving and artificial respiration were made in the year, and preliminary arrangements were being made for the formation of a Hong Kong branch of the society. This came into being on 1 January 1961, and proved to be one of the most enthusiastic — and generous — of all the overseas branches.

Trinidad and Tobago were shortly to have their own branch (formed in November 1961 with a membership of ten), and steps were taken to form a branch in Aden and Gibraltar, both instituted in January 1962. After a visit to Jamaica by the grand president, Lord Mountbatten, a branch was formed there. It seemed very likely that eventually most countries of the Commonwealth would have their own branches. The Aden branch was later closed, and reverted to the system of honorary representation, due to the absence of all-the-year-round swimming facilities.

In response to many requests, award certificates were printed in languages other than English, though the Diploma, the most highly rated of all awards and distinctions, was kept in English

ASK A SILLY QUESTION . . .

What do you call the point where land and water meet? It was a question that taxed the Countryside Commission of Scotland in 1973. They came up with an individual answer: 'A universally attractive situation for people for all sorts of purposes.'
How about 'beach'?

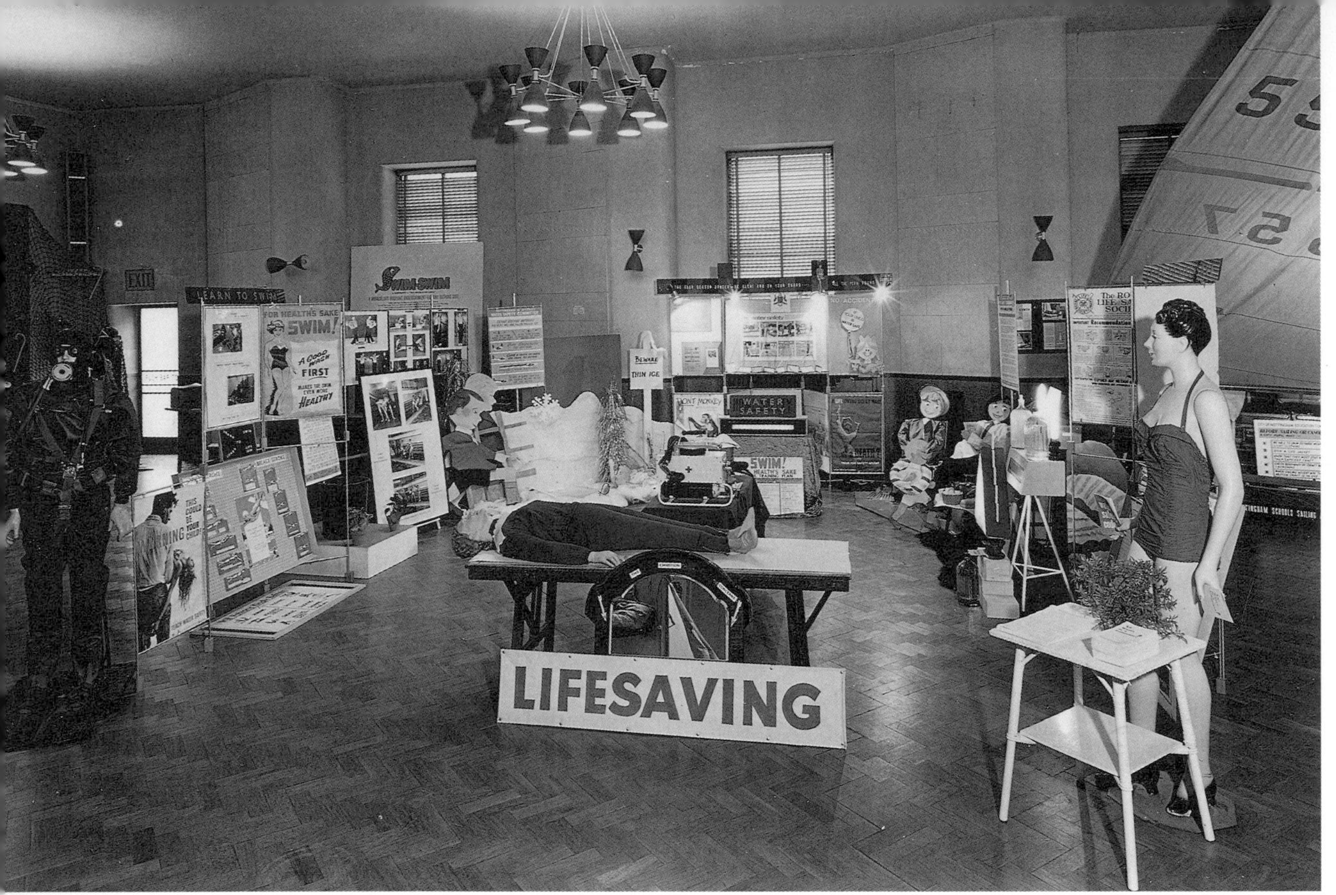

Water Safety Conference Exhibition at Nottingham in March 1965, a consequence of Lord Mountbatten's enthusiasm and desire to promote the RLSS as announced in his speech at the Commonwealth Conference in 1959

only. Because of the growth of the society and the need to maintain a close liaison between the headquarters and the national branches it was decided to appoint a deputy secretary, thus allowing either the chief secretary or the deputy secretary to visit branches without disrupting the essential work at headquarters.

At an early stage there was a crisis. South Africa decided to leave the Commonwealth, and the future of the well-attended and long-established branches in South Africa was earnestly debated. Throughout these years Lord Mountbatten travelled widely, in one year meeting members of the society from Nairobi, Mombasa, Aden, Kuala Lumpur, Singapore, Hong Kong, Canberra, Wellington, Fiji and Ottawa.

In the field of rescue and resuscitation, a new era was opening. Research work largely carried out in the United States using anaesthetised and curarized patients (those completely paralysed and not breathing) had shown the greater efficiency of the expired air method (mouth-to-mouth) over manual techniques. After consultation with their medical committee, the national executive of the RLSS reviewed the whole position in 1959. It came to the conclusion that the 'aesthetic and practical disadvantages made it unsuitable for inclusion at that time in the Society's teaching.'

What were the disadvantages? Parents of children and school authorities would find the method unacceptable. But this obstacle was partly removed first of all by the use of a plastic tube between patient and operator, and, more important, the provision of models and manikins for children and adults to practise on.

In July 1960 it was decided to hold a Commonwealth Conference in London in July 1961, and HM the Queen Mother consented to open the conference in St James's Palace. A great honour was bestowed on delegates to the conference by their being invited to a reception at Buckingham Palace. In opening the conference the Queen Mother spoke of the great importance of lifesaving, and how in the past when visiting the Commonwealth countries she had been impressed by the attention devoted to it. She recalled an exciting afternoon in 1958 when she had watched a gala by the society's sister organisation in Australia, the Surf Life Saving Association, and observed that the increasing use of boats for recreation inevitably increased the risk of casualties from drowning and made a widespread knowledge of lifesaving even more essential.

Her Majesty wisely drew attention to incidents that could have been avoided with a little forethought, and how parents should inculcate into their children the need for safe swimming and knowledge of lifesaving. Parents could do a lot in this respect, and Her Majesty felt proud that both her daughters had gained awards of the society. Regarding the Commonwealth organisation of the society she said:

STRENGTH OF PURPOSE

Mrs Adele Raymond, 56, won eleven lifesaving awards in a year, plus the RLSS Distinction Award. Perhaps nothing remarkable in this — except that Mrs Raymond is an arthritic. 'I can haul a 14-stone lifeboatman out of the pool, but pushing a vacuum cleaner around the house creases me up.'

Physical disabilities are no bar to learning water safety, and these girls from Chorley Wood College are blind or partially sighted

ELIZABETH THE SECOND by the Grace of God of the United Kingdom of Great Britain and Northern Ireland and of Our other Realms and Territories Queen, Head of the Commonwealth, Defender of the Faith.

TO ALL TO WHOM THESE PRESENTS SHALL COME, GREETING!

WHEREAS His Majesty King George the Fifth in the year of our Lord One thousand nine hundred and twenty-four by Royal Charter (hereinafter called "the original Charter") dated the fourteenth day of July in the fifteenth year of His Reign constituted the members of the Council of the Society therein named and their successors a body corporate and politic by the name of "The Royal Life Saving Society" with perpetual succession and with power to sue and be sued by that name and to use a common seal:

AND WHEREAS it has been represented to Us that it is expedient that the said Society should be reorganised so as to give a greater measure of independence to the National Branches thereof in Our United Kingdom, Canada, Australia, New Zealand and South Africa (the United Kingdom National Branch taking responsibility for all areas not within the jurisdiction of any other National Branch) and to provide for the setting up of a representative Commonwealth Council to co-ordinate the work of the National Branches and the Society as a whole:

AND WHEREAS supplication has been made unto Us to grant to the said Society a Supplemental Charter altering its present constitution for the purposes aforesaid and also for the purpose of otherwise bringing its regulations up to date:

NOW KNOW YE That We of Our Royal will and pleasure and moved thereto by Our desire to promote the work of the said Society for Ourselves, Our Heirs and Successors in addition to and notwithstanding anything to the contrary contained in the original Charter have granted, ordained and declared and by these Presents are graciously pleased to grant, ordain and declare as follows:

1. In this Our Supplemental Charter unless the context otherwise requires:

"The Society" shall mean the Royal Life Saving Society.

"The Council" shall mean the Commonwealth Council of the Society hereby constituted.

"The Bye-Laws" shall mean the Bye-Laws set forth in the Schedule hereto or other the Bye-Laws of the Society for the time being in force under or by virtue of this Our Supplemental Charter.

Words importing the singular number only shall include the plural number and vice versa, words importing the masculine gender shall include the feminine gender and words importing persons shall include corporations.

2. The Society shall have power:

(i) To purchase, take on lease or hire or otherwise acquire and hold (as regards any lands, tenements and hereditaments in England and Wales, without Licence in Mortmain) any lands, buildings, easements or hereditaments of any tenure, patents, patent rights, trade marks and any other real or personal property and to construct, provide, maintain, repair and alter any buildings, works, stores, plant and things which may from time to time be deemed requisite in any part of the Commonwealth for any of the purposes of the Society but subject as regards any lands, tenements and hereditaments within Our United Kingdom to the proviso contained in the last paragraph of this Article.

The Royal Charter and seal, in which it is stated that it is expedient that the Society should be reorganised so as to give a greater measure of independence to the branches. With this, known as the Supplemental Charter, the RLSS became a more broad-based organisation, with Canada, Australia, and New Zealand equal partners with Great Britain

'I know that the conditions of your work vary from country to country, but I am delighted to learn that above all your purpose is to keep the society as one Commonwealth body.'

As a memento of the occasion the Queen Mother graciously accepted a gold and enamel brooch in the form of the society's badge.

At the first Commonwealth Conference in 1961 it was agreed that the expired air system (EAR) should be the first method of choice in the society's teaching. In November a symposium on emergency resuscitation was held in Norway, and experts from

Heroic Rescue

1961: Dennis James McLellan of Botany Bay, New South Wales, Australia

Fourteen-year-old Dennis McLellan was fishing from the bank when he heard a call for help. A man and a boy of seventeen and some dogs were in the water. The boy had got out of his depth in a strong current from the outlet of a power-house cooling system. McLellan seized the boy, who was unconscious, by the hair and pulled him to the bank, where a girl gave him artificial respiration, and then went back for the man, who had managed to fend for himself and now in shallower water was able to wade ashore. McLellan was five feet tall and of slight build. The two he rescued were heavily built.

all over the world attended, and mouth-to-mouth resuscitation was recommended as the best technique.

In 1962 HRH the Prince of Wales gained the Elementary Certificate and the Bronze Medallion, and HRH Prince Richard of Gloucester gained the Bronze Medallion.

A signal honour was conferred on the RLSS in 1964, at Lord Mountbatten's request, when the Queen approved the addition of the Royal Crown to the society's badge. it was affirmation of the great interest the Royal Family has shown in the society since its inception.

Throughout the subsequent years the membership of the branches has continued to grow, and there is no question that the establishment of the new constitution for the RLSS has given added vigour to the overseas lifesaving organisations. Some of the Commonwealth branches have faced conditions unknown to the UK branch. In 1963 Hong Kong suffered an acute water shortage and training was necessarily cut down; there was also a lack of pools and beaches for training. It is worth remembering that Hong Kong is only eleven miles long and two and a half miles wide. In Hong Kong and neighbouring Kowloon the population was four million, and there were only fifty major beaches, which were always crowded. Some of the requirements had to be amended, such as diving from a height. Conditions for examination were not good; at one pool 25m long 145 persons had to be examined within two hours.

In Kenya there was a lack of suitable places for training and examinations. There were only two swimming pools in the whole

BOY SCOUTS

Lifesaving first appeared in the Boy Scouts' curriculum in 1910. The Rescuer Badge was awarded to boys who could swim 50yd in clothing, fling a lifeline or lifebelt 20ft, and who could demonstrate the rescue from drowning of a person and how to revive that person. Perhaps the demands on young boys were too much; in 1914 the distance to be swum was reduced to 10yd.

In 1961 it was agreed that the Expired Air Resuscitation method should be the first choice in the teaching of the RLSS

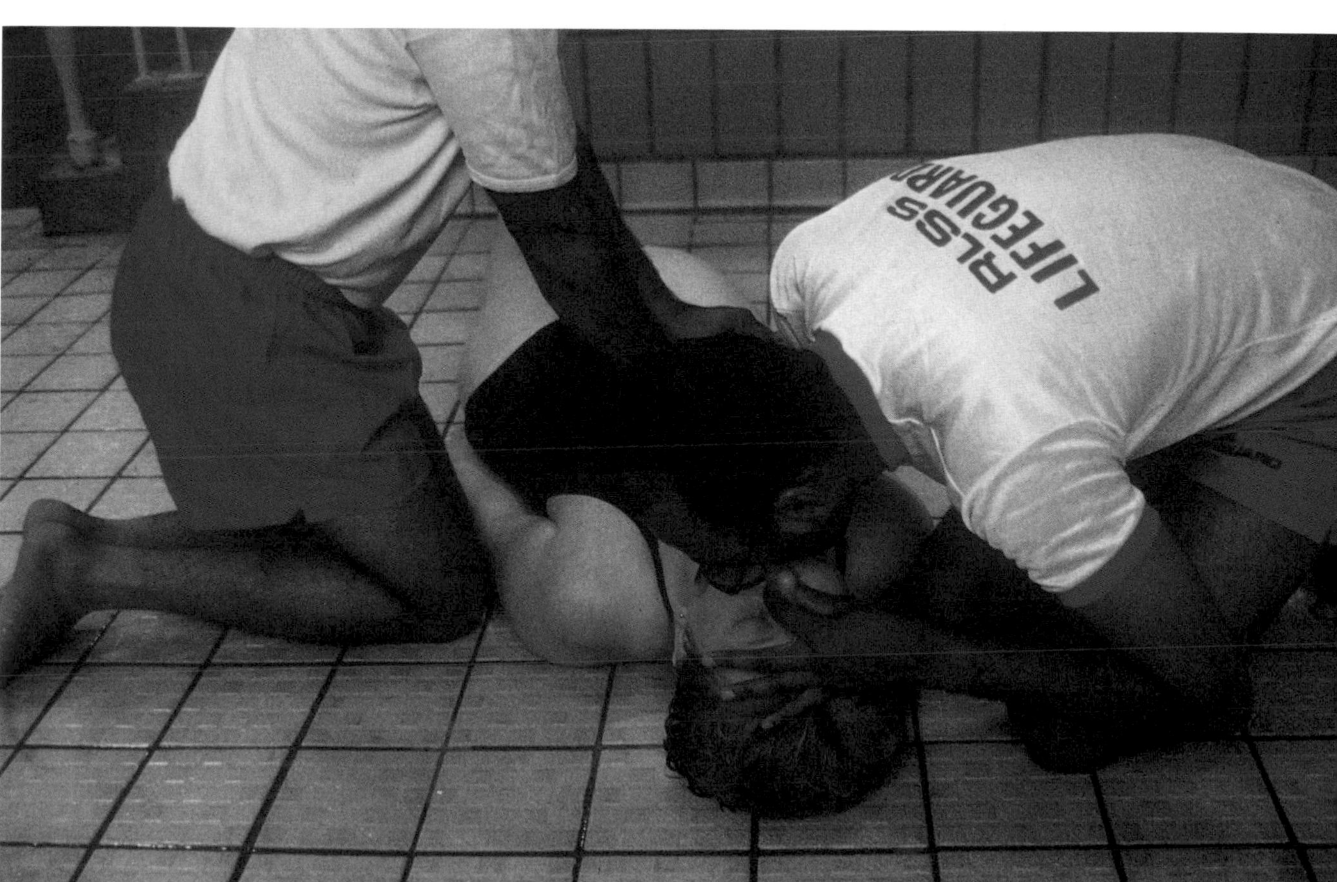

A LONG WAY UP

A hundred years ago the plunge was a popular competitive sport. In 1888 G. A. Blake (amateur) did 75ft 7in at Lambeth Baths.

of the country outside the capital, Nairobi. There was only one swimming pool in Nairobi for Africans or Asians, and then only if they belonged to the Boy Scouts or the Girl Guides.

In some Commonwealth countries much depended on the availability of direct government assistance. In Jamaica the representative at the 1966 Commonwealth Conference admitted that 'as yet the competition has not gained the magnitude we would like because of lack of teachers who can assist in training'.

It was clear that some Commonwealth branches were having a particularly difficult time. Nigeria, with 55 million people, was one of them. The representative was quite open about the reasons as he told the audience that of the country's population 'only about ten per cent enjoy anything like the standard of living that any of you here enjoys.' Although there was enthusiasm there was no money. He explained why succinctly and persuasively:

> 'There is a Committee in Lagos called Lagos Lifeguard Advisory Committee, represented by the Boy Scouts, St John's, The Red Cross, the Minister of Education, the Police, and honorary representatives of the society (RLSS). They receive a grant of about £600 a year, but we spend that entirely on eight professional lifeguards, who work on the two beaches in Lagos. They do excellent work and they save hundreds of lives in a year.'

The average wage for an able-bodied male such as a police recruit was £3 a week, and such a person could not afford a bathing costume, a handbook, a badge, or the swimming pool charges. Far less the schoolchildren who would be the greatest beneficiaries and whose involvement in lifesaving schemes was essential.

There were other problems, for although handbooks had been translated from English, as well as certificates and awards, 'quite frankly, the first-aid part of our handbook is very much beyond about three-quarters of the people who apply . . . I do not know what can be done to simplify the technical terminology or how far it is really necessary . . . I think that quite a lot of the terminology is unnecessarily technical and too far advanced'. This judgment may have applied as well to other branches than Nigeria.

Heroic Rescue

1962: Hilary Westerman of Scarcroft Grange, Leeds, Yorkshire

Fifteen-year-old Miss Westerman rescued a woman from a park lake, formerly a quarry, which was thirty feet deep, and in which, because of the filthy water and uncertain hazards, bathing was forbidden. The woman was unconscious and floating downwards in the water, her face blue. Despite being frightened, Miss Westerman brought the woman to the bank, where a man from a boat helped to land her. Although very exhausted, Miss Westerman gave manual resuscitation for ten minutes until relieved by a park ranger.

One way to put over information in an easily understood fashion is the poster. The results of a poster competition on behalf of the RLSS. There is no question that they all deserved to be used

So far as Nigeria was concerned, the need was a person in authority. Such people 'are already claimed by the amateur theatrical society, the Scouts, Olympic Associations or St John's. They are all looking for chairmen of the type that we want for our honorary representatives.'

This was certainly not a problem peculiar to Nigeria, nor indeed the RLSS.

One answer to money problems in the poorer branches was support by those which were richer. Australia had sent free equipment to Nigeria, Canada was willing to take a bigger share of the responsibility in helping the growth and development of the society in the Caribbean countries. It was agreed that visiting technical officers would be a great help in sorting out some uncertain areas and in clearing up doubts about training programmes.

Occasionally politics interfered with established routines. In what was Southern Rhodesia the break-up of the Federation obliged many leading figures in the lifesaving scene to leave, and the changing borders meant that Nyasaland was no longer represented.

But however uncertain the political situation has been in Commonwealth countries, the work of the lifesavers has continued to flourish. And Lord Mountbatten travelled throughout the Commonwealth, encouraging and persuading. In 1964 he personally presented the Mountbatten Medal to Lynda Dann from Alberta, a fifteen-year-old girl who rescued a ten-year-old girl from treacherous waters with a risk of being swept into a nearby whirlpool. Of thirty bystanders she was the only one capable of effecting a rescue. The congratulations of HM Queen Elizabeth II were later conveyed to Miss Dann. It was the second year in succession that the winner of the Mountbatten Medal had been awarded to someone from Alberta.

In Britain a film was completed, *To Match Your Courage,* once again demonstrating the society's intention to foster its public image. A quarterly journal was introduced to replace the headquarters newsletter, in which material from all the branches worldwide was presented with enviable professionalism.

The second Quinquennial Commonwealth Conference coincided with seventy-five years of the RLSS. It was opened at St James's Palace on 18 July 1966 by HRH the Princess Margaret, and in the evening HM the Queen and the Duke of Edinburgh gave a

Cartoon characters were brought in to push the message of water safety

The moment that counts – bringing the casualty ashore

reception at Buckingham Palace. Lord Mountbatten gave a reception at the House of Lords, and on another evening delegates were guests of Lord Mountbatten and Sir Solly Zuckerman at the Zoological Gardens. On the Saturday delegates travelled to Broadlands, Lord Mountbatten's home, where they were shown round the house and gardens. The progress of the RLSS in all its aspects was confirmed. As Princess Margaret declared, the total number of proficiency awards issued by the society had now passed the five million mark, 'a great tribute to voluntary workers everywhere and to the vision and foresight of your founder.'

It was indeed. Princess Margaret went on to say that there was no room for complacency, nor could there be until every child of school age was taught how to swim and how to act in an emergency. Seven hundred deaths by drowning a year was still too high a figure. And that was just in the United Kingdom.

Lord Mountbatten emphasised the need to be progressive, and pointed out the problems of facilities and lack of pools. These problems must have been very obvious during his Commonwealth tours when he was spreading the lifesaving gospel.

'We need', he announced, 'the weapon of propaganda to

A SMALL PROBLEM

In 1665 50 people in London drowned, 68,596 died of the plague. As one writer said, drowning 'was a very small problem.'

Opposite:
The RLSS float in the Lord Mayor's Show , putting the society increasingly in the public eye

improve the situation.' He did not believe that voluntary service, despite what others said, was on the decline:

> What we as a society must do is to seek the help of the service of young people of good character, to welcome them as teachers and leaders and to offer them the challenge of service in our own society. We shall have failed ourselves and them if we do not achieve this. We cannot count on them to come to us. We must do the seeking.

They were wise words for a new age, the age of admass, the age of propaganda. The long-established voluntary organisations, often drawing their recruits in a haphazard manner by word of mouth, were all inclined to go on as they had done in the past. But not the RLSS. Lord Mountbatten was followed by Sir Henry Studdy, CBE, the national president of the United Kingdom branch. He emphasised his belief in progress. Too many people were unaware of what the RLSS meant:

> 'Our aim is to look to the future, to make our work better known to the public, many of whom seem to think that we are concerned with lifeboats.'

To mark seventy-five years of the RLSS there were numerous celebratory events, including demonstrations, an exhibition backed by the *Daily Mail* — and the Surrey branch of the RLSS won a trophy at the annual Battersea Easter Parade.

'We need the weapon of propaganda to improve the situation', said Lord Mountbatten. How about this, a marvellous action photograph captioned 'Jump (in)to it! They've capsized and are drowning!'

Heroic Rescue

1963: Kenneth David Howlett of Edmonton, Alberta, Canada

Howlett was driving a car with friends in early December when he saw three boys in difficulty on ice near a river bank. One boy aged three was pulled out by one of Howlett's companions, but a four-year-old boy was drifting downstream face downwards. It was clear that there was no time to be lost. Howlett stripped off most of his clothing and made a lifeline of shirts and belts and other suitable clothing. This was not long enough, so despite the freezing temperatures he swam to the boy, brought him to shore, and gave him mouth-to-mouth resuscitation while clinging to the edge of the ice.

OVERDRESSED

'Bathing is best performed when quite naked but decency forbids entire nudity, a kind of short drawers is worn; and where ladies and gentlemen bathe in company, as is the fashion all along the Atlantic coast, shirts and trowsers are worn.'

Swimming, by J. W. and N. Orr. New York, 1846

The Lifeguard Corps held its first annual conference at Bognor Regis, with the emphasis on expansion and strengthening. That was the aim throughout the RLSS, at home and abroad.

Lord Mountbatten must have been gratified as he looked back at the formative years of the reconditioned and reorganised RLSS, much of its prestige and success due to him and his strenuous efforts, often combined with an intensive public programme, to promote it by visiting not only the main national branches, but the newcomers to the league, those starting up with barely a dozen members.

A sad event was recorded in 1967 with the death of the chief secretary, Capt A. E. Biscoe after twenty years' sterling service. He had seen a great many changes, and there were more to come as the restructuring of the organisation in the UK proceeded. The Lifeguard Corps was expanding, and there were eighty-three clubs manning sixty-four posts.

The RLSS was constantly establishing new links. It joined the Federation International de Sauvetage and teams competed in international competitions.

The Third Quinquennial Conference was opened at Marlborough House on 12 July 1971 by HRH Princess Alexandra. Since the last meeting Malaysia had been granted national branch status, and the grand president had attended the inaugural ceremony in Kuala Lumpur. A branch had been formed in Singapore, one of the new high-fliers in the Commonwealth. A novel feature of the conference was the staging of the first ever lifesaving match in the United Kingdom under international rules, with teams from France and Spain contending with teams from Britain.

All the guests agreed that there was increasing pressure on lakes, rivers, and coastal waters. Skin and scuba diving had become mass sports in the richer countries, as had water skiing and power-boat usage. Increased leisure in some countries had led to an upsurge in specialised sport, such as snowmobiling in Canada, much of it carrying an element of danger. The Canadian representative drew attention to social changes, occurring there as well as everywhere else. Education in lifesaving, as in everything

Heroic Rescue

1964: Miss Lynda Ruth Dann of Vulcan, Alberta, Canada

A twelve-year-old boy and a ten-year-old girl were wading in a creek and suddenly slipped into deep water. The boy's father, a non-swimmer, managed to push the boy towards a bystander and he was pulled to safety. He and the girl then disappeared. Miss Dann, aged fifteen, removed her shoes and swam to the rescue despite strong currents and the danger of being swept into a nearby whirlpool. She rescued the girl, and searched for the man for three-quarters of an hour, finally recovering him, dead, from eight feet of water. Unfortunately there were thirty bystanders who could not do anything to assist.

else, must be handled differently. 'We must sell our programme', he said, 'rather than merely offer it. Such an approach takes personnel and money.'

The Canadian representative, Lt Gen .G. G. Simonds, also made some pertinent remarks on the question of finance, mentioning that the body most associated with RLSS Canada was the Water Safety Service of the Canadian Red Cross Society. The Water Safety Service received $700,000 (£280,000) a year; RLSS Canada existed on examination fees, the sale of literature, and nominal grants. Gen Simonds thought that there should be a revaluation of the whole lifesaving programme, and produced some interesting statistics. In 1970 there had been 1,275 drownings in a country of 23 million; of these only 207 were the result of swimming accidents. A third of the fatalities arose from incidents involving boats.

Conditions in the various Commonwealth countries naturally vary, but no doubt the general's remarks applied with equal validity to those countries which enjoy a high standard of living with ample opportunities for expensive leisure activities. With 95 per cent of the water activities in Canada concerned with inland waters, the reverse was the case in Australia. In Australia safety on the beaches was frequently in the capable hands of the Surf Life Saving Association, though the Victoria branch of RLSS Australia covered about forty beaches. RLSS Australia was mostly involved with ports, bays, harbours, rivers and inland waters. Similarly the New Zealand Surf Life Saving Association (created by a resolution of the RLSS New Zealand council in 1932) was the sole body concerned with the beaches. The equipment available to the 3,000 active members included Jeeps, three-wheeled vehicles, jet-boats and a helicopter. A far cry from the equipment available to the smaller RLSS branches.

Lord Mountbatten did not live to see the future development of the grand scheme. His tragic death was a great blow to not only the country but to the society to which he had been so committed, Others have done what they can to fill the gap. But his example has been difficult to follow. Some would say impossible.

THE FIRST SURF BOARD

In a periodical published in 1847 there is reference to a 'swimming skate invented in France a few years ago.' This might very well be the first reference to the surf board in Europe.

Heroic Rescue

1966: Terrence H. Scorer of Western Australia

A man and his twelve-year-old son were looking for somewhere to fish. The sea was rough with a heavy swell. They were standing on rocks fifteen feet above sea level when a wave washed the man down a blowhole, under a reef, and into the sea. He remained calm, but knew he could not reach the shore unaided. When seen by Scorer he was 600yd out. Scorer put on flippers, waited for a suitable wave which would take him over the reef, knowing that it would be difficult to get back without help. Despite the possible presence of sharks, he managed to get the man to the reef, by which time bystanders had improvised a rope. After much difficulty and danger, even to the men on the rope, the man was brought ashore. The rescuer was in the water for over an hour.

1972 – 91 The Challenge of Today

On 22 November 1972 Admiral of the Fleet, the Earl Mountbatten of Burma retired as Grand President after twenty-seven years in office, and HRH Princess Alexandra was graciously pleased to accept the office. Earl Mountbatten looked back at his years in office, declaring that the best yardstick of progress was the annual total of proficiency awards gained. In 1945 there had been 86,000; in 1971 there had been 472,000.

Another indication of progress was the decrease in the number of drownings throughout the countries of the Commonwealth. Typical of the effect of the work of the RLSS in both lifesaving and education was in New Zealand, where the rate of drowning accidents had gone down from 16.4 per 100,000 in 1910 to 4.6. Although not one of the largest branches, New Zealand had been one of the most progressive, producing its own handbook in 1965 (13,000 sold in the first year), and had taken over responsibility in the Cook Islands and Fiji, as well as sending a team to Sri Lanka to demonstrate and instruct to Bronze Medallion standard.

As the years had gone by, there had been increasing collaboration between the various safety organisations, not only in the UK but throughout the Commonwealth. The YMCA adopted the awards programme of RLSS Canada as its standard for lifesaving, and this was just one example as it was generally realised that the methods of the RLSS throughout the Commonwealth, no matter how they might differ in detail, could not be bettered.

In the UK the 'Learn to Lifesave' scheme of 1974 was handsomely supported by all, and the involvement of business in sponsorship was widely welcomed. Mobil Oil Company Ltd had very generously backed the Lifeguard Corps, and valuable equipment had been provided for clubs, together with an excellent recruiting film.

With local government reorganisation it was necessary to restructure the branches in the United Kingdom, and many were

THE NEW VIKINGS

In 1979 the Isle of Man celebrated the Millennium of Tynwald, a thousand years of self-government and to mark the occasion a replica Viking ship was built in Norway and sailed 1,800 miles along the old Viking route to Man, the ancient centre of their Kingdom of the Western Isles.

A mixed crew of Norwegians and Manxmen faced the rigours of the North Sea and the wild waters around the north of Scotland, with near disaster when the longship capsized. The eleven crew members from the Isle of Man were well trained in survival techniques, and all were successful in acquiring their Bronze medallions. Their survival was a tribute not only to their guts but to their common sense.

Lord Mountbatten inspecting a display team from the Life Guard Corps (as it was called then)

renamed. For the first time the annual total of Commonwealth awards passed the half-million mark. But there was still more to do. The RLSS UK Rescue Skills Scheme, sponsored by the National Westminster Bank in 1975, got off to a healthy start, and the 50,000th award winner, Angela Smith, was featured in the BBC TV children's programme *Blue Peter*.

The Commonwealth Conference of 1976 once again brought representatives from many countries to the conference table, not afraid to tackle the problems of the day, including hyper-inflation and the need to function on severely restricted budgets, The President of RLSS Canada, Mr R. Bredin Stapells, QC, asked many searching questions of his colleagues and associates. One of these was, 'Why do people work for the Royal Life Saving Society?' It was a difficult question. One of the leaders in Canada, said the Canadian president, warned, 'Don't ask that question, we may find the answer and it may be a mistake.'

One of the most successful of the postwar schemes was the Blue Code with its imaginative logo, and it is interesting to see that the prizes for the Blue Code Water Watch Competition of 1983 were what children wanted – computers

You can lead a crocodile to water, but can you make it think?

Enter your class, youth group, scout group, or children's group for the

Blue Code Water Watch Competition

and they could win a COMMODORE COMPUTER.

Mr Bredin Stapells went on to say that the RLSS depended on volunteers. 'No volunteers — no programme — no society.'

'Arising from the volunteers' scene,' he continued, 'one of the things which we have seen over and over again is that volunteers only work in fits and starts, by and large, because they have other duties; they have to earn their living for instance... so, the obvious answer is that you have got to have some full-time professional staff.' In Canada, the use of full-time paid staff resulted in a 30 per cent expansion of the programme.

There was a danger, as he had seen in other organisations, that 'a large staff of people on the payroll sometimes kills the involvement of the volunteer. If it does that, it's a mistake, isn't it? At least that's what we have said around our tables before. So this is an area we ought to give some thought to. What is the right mix?'

BABY IN TOW

During the National Finals in Coventry during the early 1970s, all competitors had been drilled 'Whatever you do, you *must take an aid* . . . avoid contact at all cost, *you must use an aid.*'

An incident for the schoolgirls consisted of a drowning mother and baby, plus two or three other people needing help in various ways. One of the rescuers quickly moved towards the mother and baby, saying 'Keep calm, I am a trained lifesaver!' She rescued the baby, and swam towards the mother. 'Grab hold of this — hold on tight — use two hands!' she called out.

A look of relief could be seen on the rescuer's face — she had avoided contact and used an aid. Good marks, she thought as she swam for shore. But what was the towing aid? The baby!

Esme Wilson

The Canadian president went on to the question of finance. He declared that RLSS Canada did not want to be a creature of the government, but money had to be found somehow. As in many other branches, money was forthcoming from examination forms and fees, but there was a limit as to how much one could charge. And the same was true with lifesaving literature. Canada was also contemplating an involvement in retailing safety equipment, as well as the possibility of organising lotteries to raise money. He also paid tribute to the administrative role of the United Kingdom in uncompromising terms:

'Why is it that we can sit here and expect the UK to carry the whole darn load?'

One of the major papers read at the conference was prepared by RLSS Canada, and concerned the future of the RLSS. The first question asked was whether the RLSS should try to move into counties outside the Commonwealth. 'How can we adapt our lifesaving programme to other cultures not preconditioned or receptive to our concerns?' Of course there were three existing international societies — World Life Saving, the Federation Internationale de Sauvetage (FIS), and the Red Cross (which operated mainly in the United States and Bulgaria). Some countries were members of both World Life Saving and the FIS, the published goals of which were similar, and there were countries that had separate organisations for different activities.

While the disparity between advanced countries and Third World countries was as wide as ever, it was asked whether RLSS

A GOOD HAUL

A typical year's tally by the South Hams (Devon) Lifeguards. In 1988 they rescued 25 sail-boarders, 23 surfers, 17 people on inflatables, and 13 swimmers. They also rescued 6 people cut off by the tide, and there were 7 boat emergencies.

'No volunteers, no programmes, no society.' This applies to teachers as well as lifeguards and examiners

SAFETY LAST

'It is disturbing to see people spending large sums of money on an expensive dinghy or yacht and yet skimping on essential safety equipment. They simply don't understand that the sea can be very unforgiving and that if you make a mistake you may not get another chance.'

Leader in the *Greenock Telegraph*, January 1989

programmes were available to all, and whether the RLSS realised the significance of the explosion of outdoor activities. It was projected that the working week would get shorter and shorter, giving more opportunities for adventurous leisure. It was predicted that the working week would drop from 40 hours in 1965 to 22 hours in 1985, although this has not happened. Nor has the average retirement age dropped to 38 in 1985, as was anticipated. It was supposed that with this increased leisure, it would be easier to attract volunteers — if the work were sufficiently stimulating.

RLSS UK rejected the proposal that the RLSS should go worldwide, and emphasised that it was essentially a Commonwealth organisation, and that the FIS could do the best job in Europe. A suggestion that the name of the RLSS should be changed was also turned down, and it was also predicted that the changes in working hours and retirement would not be nearly so drastic as anticipated by the Canadian president. RLSS UK was perfectly right.

It was also put forward in the discussion that there should be a central body to give rulings that all the bodies in the RLSS would observe. This was roundly rejected. The Australia president pointed out that in his own country each of the six states was autonomous and was not bound to accept the rulings of the national council. Centralisation, he said, meant stagnation.

The New Zealand delegation was in favour of retaining the existing overall structure and in keeping the RLSS a purely Commonwealth concern, though developing countries, where there was no arrangement for a lifesaving force at all, should be encouraged to seek help and advice from technical officers, or those 'who have gone as far as they can in their own branch and for whom the ordinary instruction and examination starts to pall. Sometimes these people are prepared to travel and find out

Heroic Rescue

1978: George Geddes Parsonage of Glasgow

In the early hours of an April morning, a 43-year-old woman threw herself into the River Clyde from the Albert Bridge in Glasgow. The river depth at this point was between 8 and 12ft and an additional hazard was constituted by the remains of the metal structure of a former bridge projecting from the river bed into the fast flowing waters. George Geddes Parsonage was awoken from sleep and rushed to the bridge, where Insp Kenneth McLean and Sgt Colin Campbell of the Strathclyde Police were in attendance. Parsonage dropped a lifebuoy into the river, securing its retaining line on the parapet of the bridge. The police officers then lowered him some 60ft into the river by means of a second rope. In the pitch darkness and with the water temperature at 2°C, he swam 6yd to the woman and returned her by a chin tow to the rope end at his point of entry into the water. Her unconscious body caught on the parapet as it was raised on the rope by the police officers. Parsonage was himself raised by the second line to free her, before she was finally brought to safety. Although by this time he was very much fatigued he applied artificial respiration and, within less than a minute, the woman's breathing re-started and she was removed to hospital by ambulance.

whether we could further the knowledge of the Royal Life Society techniques with individual nations.' Such altruistic persons would not find it over-difficult to get subsidised air fares from international air lines.

The question of a change of title was raised several times. RLSS UK emphasised the goodwill that existed, and which could be lost with a different name. But why should anyone want the name changed? Mr Teoh Teck Lee of Malaysia said that newly independent Commonwealth countries had become sovereign states, and branches found that it was a delicate matter when asking for government aid to an organisation with such a title, which to many of the new rulers had an aura of the old British Empire. (Malaysia dropped the 'Royal' from its name in 1984.)

Be that as it may, Capt E. Hale, director of RLSS UK until 1965 when he retired and at one time a close naval associate of Lord Mountbatten, pointed out a singular difficulty. When the second Royal Charter was promulgated, Captain Hale had asked the Clerk of the Privy Council about the possibility of a change of name and had been categorically informed that there was no possibility of a new title without losing the Royal Charter.

All branches agreed that the RLSS needed a strong image to ensure that volunteers would continue to come forward. In projecting the image of the society professional help was used,

It was projected that by 1985 the working week would be down to 22 hours, leaving vast leisure time, with water-based activities bound to dramatically increase

A lifesaving group in Cyprus. Throughout the hundred years of the Royal Life Saving Society there has been an emphasis on carrying the message to all the corners of the world

including that of the giant advertising agency Saatchi and Saatchi in the UK. RLSS Australia had the problem that surf lifesaving, which had its own organisation, attracted the most media attention because of the glamour associated with surfing and surf rescue, and that, although the RLSS was fully supported by its brother association, many ordinary people found it difficult to identify with its educational work.

The Australian delegation drew attention to the amazing increase in what were described as 'private backyard pools'. In one season 100,000 new ones had been constructed, and in view of the increasing number of drownings of children in these swimming pools thousands of parents were desperate for knowledge of resuscitation, putting great pressure on the facilities offered by the state branches.

One of the great advantages to all delegates at the Commonwealth Conferences was the availability of information on new techniques and new discoveries. Included in the new technology of 1976 was the product of a company called Laerdal, a manikin, which had a recording mechanism inside to give a print-out

Spinal injuries were also being caused by new features such as the flume in water-leisure centres

telling the operator whether he or she had done sufficient ventilating or sufficient compression. A wide variety of new resuscitators was also available. The torpedo buoy, so long the basic piece of rescue equipment in open water, was being looked at afresh. In Canada it was being rendered obsolete by the rescue tube, which could be hooked round a victim, and the rescue can, which had a shape similar to the rescue tube but was fitted with handles.

Over the years it had been found increasingly that not enough attention was devoted to spinal injuries caused by diving into shallow water, falling while water skiing, and being knocked into the bottom on surf beaches. Skiing and surfing were relatively unknown when the earlier handbooks on lifesaving were pub-

The emphasis in recent years has been on selfless and adventurous promotion. This excellent display dates from 1983

STANDING ROOM ONLY

'They were letting in swarms of people. There was standing room only in the water. You can't expect the attendants to supervise so many people. How could they see if someone was in trouble?

'We were very upset at seeing the boy pulled out. He was blue in the face and we thought he might be dead.'

The wave machine was criticised. Young children were jostled against the sides of the swimming bath and into each other by the force of the waves.

'There was an announcement for non-swimmers to clear the deep end when the machine was switched on, but you could hardly hear it above all the noise and commotion.'

Eyewitness at new leisure centre pool in Sussex, in 1988

lished, and little comment had been made on spinal injury.

It was emphasised that with a spinal injury there should be a minimum of three or four reasonably competent assistants for a trained rescuer, and that it was vitally necessary to immobilise the spine. If the victim was not breathing, mouth-to-mouth resuscitation would need to be carried out carefully, lifting the jaw so that there should be no further damage to the neck.

It had been a very productive Commonwealth Conference and, with the increasing integration between the branches, the titles of Grand President and Deputy Grand President were changed to Commonwealth President and Deputy Commonwealth President in 1977. In the UK, the Lifeguard Corps was renamed the RLSS Lifeguards, and shortly afterwards the National Lifeguard Championship was honoured by the presence of Royalty. The Rescue Skills Scheme in the UK was still going well, and the 100,000th award winner, Matthew Baker, received a presentation watch from the sponsors. Another scheme was started, the Safe Swimmer campaign, but the year 1979 was clouded by the tragic assassination of Lord Mountbatten.

In 1980 there was a new start. The RLSS purchased the freehold of the seventeenth-century Manor House in Studley, Warwickshire, with the intention of converting it into its UK and Commonwealth Headquarters. Three months were spent putting in central heating, rewiring, and the conversion of the stable block and coach house into the Awards and Sales Department. The sale of the leasehold on Desborough House in London was completed, and removal to Warwickshire followed shortly.

Right: Crowds waiting in Studley for the arrival of the Queen Mother to open Mountbatten House

Prince Michael of Kent receiving an engraved silver spade from the Clerk to Studley Parish Council, Mr J. W. Clarke, before planting a commemorative tree in the gardens of Mountbatten House

With the backing of the planning authority, the Stratford-on-Avon District Council and the department of the Environment, the building work and the necessary repairs were done with great taste to fit in with this marvellous building. With the support of the RLSS members throughout the UK and the Commonwealth, charitable trusts, and industry and commerce £90,000 was raised to help in the conversion, much of it devoted to the Hong Kong Room, a large airy room that replaced a lean-to Victorian conservatory. The RLSS is eternally in the debt of the Hong Kong branch for their sterling contribution to the Headquarters, named, naturally, Mountbatten House and opened by HM The Queen Mother on 25 June 1981 (the anniversary of Lord Mountbatten's birthday in 1900) in the presence of 400 guests from all over the world.

Mountbatten House is not only a splendid place to work from, but it also acts as a magnet to thousands of RLSS members from all over the world. It represents not only the country from which

Heroic Rescue

1980: John Potts of Armagh, Northern Ireland

On Sunday 16 November 1980, a group of canoeists on a Senior Instructor Course were negotiating a difficult V-shaped weir on the River Blackwater at Benburb, Co Armagh, Northern Ireland. At 2.30pm, one of the canoeists, Patrick J. Grant, misjudged the point at which he was to 'shoot' the weir and his canoe was sucked from under him in the 30ft 45° weir drop. Though wearing a buoyancy aid, Grant was held in the 'stopper' wave at the foot of the weir for a short while before escaping from it in a semi-conscious state. The river was in full spate and it began to carry him downstream towards the next weir which had a vertical 20ft drop. Another member of the course, John Potts, having successfully negotiated the first weir, observed his colleague being swept away. Without thought for his own safety, he swam across the flow and caught Grant by the top of his buoyancy aid. Both were now only some 20yd from the second weir but Potts managed to tow Grant 35yd to the bank across the direction of flow of the river. Grant's breathing was difficult as he was landed but Potts gave priority to running back upstream to warn the remainder of the party of the dangers of the weir.

Presentation of the 1979 Mountbatten Medal to Patrick Farge of RLSS New Zealand by HRH the Prince of Wales

1979: Patrick Marie Bernard Farge of Whangarei, New Zealand

On a June evening, a car with four occupants crashed through a roadside barrier at Riverside Drive, Whangarei Town Basin, and entered the water upside down. Hearing the noise of the crash, Patrick Marie Bernard Farge, with his father, Paul Farge, left their trimaran *Tanea* by its dinghy and arrived on the scene within a minute or so; only the bottoms of the wheels of the crashed car were visible. One of the occupants of the car struggled free by himself and told Patrick and his father of the three still inside the vehicle. Patrick, aged 16 and a student, immediately entered the muddy water and dived repeatedly into the vehicle to release the three occupants. On at least two occasions, his clothing became trapped but he freed himself each time and continued with the rescue. The last casualty to be recovered on this dark winter's night was brought to the surface some six minutes after the crash; the efforts of PC Stephen Cook and of the ambulance crew subsequently failed to revive him, however. The remaining three casualties were treated in hospital for shock.

the RLSS sprang, but tradition at its best. It is believed to have been built in 1684, probably for Thomas Chambers. In 1727 it was known as New Hall, Studley. It is built mostly of red brick with stone facings and Ionic columns surmounted by stone vases. It is totally symmetrical except for the addition of a Victorian kitchen wing.

Old as the house is, the interior has oak panelling of a much earlier date brought from Studley Castle, one aspect of which can be seen through the trees from the rear of Mountbatten House.

The new headquarters would:

'provide the modern base which the Society now needs for the direction, expansion and support of its work of education and service.'

These were the words of the Commonwealth President, HRH Prince Michael of Kent.

A new era had begun. There was still great work to be done. But, with increased public awareness and sponsorship, lifesaving was brought home to everybody, one of the most important events in the UK being the establishment of the Blue Code for water safety.

An in-depth study of the awareness of the Blue Code among children was carried out in November 1982 by David Williams and Ketchum Ltd. Only 4 per cent of the children questioned were

WATER POLO

In 1870 a committee was appointed to draw up a code for 'football in the water.' In America as late as 1877 this was known as 'ornamental swimming'. In 1876 The Bournemouth Premier Rowing Club played 'aquatic handball.' Thus the early days of water polo.

Below far left : The Queen Mother in the grounds of Mountbatten House with a portrait of herself

A recipe for disaster, an animated conversation, perhaps a little horseplay . . .

Heroic Rescue

1981: Evan Franklin Davies of Rhyl, Wales

In August, at the West Parade, Rhyl, Clwyd, North Wales, Paul Doran (aged 16) from Liverpool entered the sea to swim. The sea was rough and a Force 6 north-westerly wind was blowing the spring high tide onto and over the sea wall. When Doran got into difficulties, his two friends, Alan Carson (aged 18) and Neil Michael Savage (aged 19), entered the water in an attempt to save him. Two beach lifeguards employed by Rhuddlan Borough Council, Evan Franklin Davies (aged 23) and Derek Denton (aged 28), on patrol observed all three youths being swept out of their depth. Whilst Denton entered the water to rescue a conscious casualty, Davies summoned help using his personal radio, then entered the water to rescue and resuscitate one of the casualties who appeared unconscious; he was unable to complete this rescue due to the prevailing conditions without the help of a lifeline brought from the shore by Denton. All three casualties were given Expired Air Resuscitation and, with the two rescuers, were subsequently treated in hospital.

---

spontaneously aware of the Blue Code and its relation to water or water safety. When the children were shown the frontispiece of the Blue Code leaflet with its distinctive and imaginative logo the level of awareness went up a further 13 per cent.

In 1983 the Commonwealth Technical Advisory Committee met in Ottawa, and the committee agreed that a more dynamic and active role for the CTAC was needed. It was established as a forum for discussion and the review of technical aspects of RLSS programmes. In an increasingly computerised society, sharing of up-to-date information was becoming easier. But it was important that this information was relevant — and understandable. For as the number of Commonwealth branches increased throughout the world it was more and more necessary to tailor the data to the audience.

In response to a recommendation of the 1976 Commonwealth Conference, regional groupings provided the opportunity for regular gatherings between the quinquennial conferences, and members of the Asia Pacific Region met in successive years in Hong Kong (1978), Penang (1979), and Singapore (1980). The first formal meeting of the Asia Pacific Life Saving Council met in Brisbane, Australia, in 1983. These delegates were thus enabled to concentrate on matters peculiar to their own areas.

Politics continued to have an effect on lifesaving in the Commonwealth, and despite enthusiasm by the nation's director of sport, it was found that the RLSS branch in Zambia had no official status. In Uganda, after a gap of ten years, lifesaving was revived. Of the non-branch countries served by Commonwealth Headquarters, Saudi Arabia had the largest number of examiners, and other Gulf states such as the United Arab Emirates and the Sultanate of Oman were becoming more interested in the question of lifesaving. In the United Arab Emirates there were seventeen drownings on a one-mile stretch of beach in 1982.

Following a complete evaluation of their award schemes, RLSS

JUST WALKED AWAY

Carl, a nine-year-old cub scout from Stanley, County Durham, was on holiday in Spain in 1988, and while by the hotel swimming pool realised that a boy of about his own age had failed to resurface.

'He ran to his mother, who didn't believe him at first', said his grandfather. 'Then she called a Spanish waiter over, but he just walked away. Then some Spanish girls dived in but they didn't want to know either, and eventually a Cockney lad pulled the boy out. . . if Carl had walked away like some of the adults did, that boy would have died.'

Incredible? Isn't it?

Australia launched their 'Swim and Survive' programme in 1983. This was a comprehensive package of water safety, swimming and survival skills, and other branches followed this lead. The UK Aquapack programme was launched in September 1984, and was an immediate success. It was Britain's first complete programme of water safety, safer swimming and rescue skills, a personal logbook in which the candidates plot their own progress through the various skills in each award and get the certificates signed as soon as they have done them.

There are two levels of Aquapack, one taking a non-swimmer to a level where he or she has a range of survival skills. The second requires candidates to demonstrate a high level of swimming ability and survival skills, an appreciation of personal water safety, and awareness of the dangers of cold water immersion, first brought to the fore by naval experts and emphasised at almost every conference on lifesaving since. Candidates who reach an advanced level qualify for the Aquagold award, and are entitled to attend a special regional presentation to receive an Aquagold lapel badge.

Encouraged by the success of these programmes in Australia and the UK, New Zealand produced its version in 1986, Malaysia in 1987, and Canada and Singapore in 1989. Variously entitled Aquacode, Aquapass, Aquapack and Aquapac, these have proved their sterling worth time and time again.

Another success is the RLSS UK summer school, which covers a wide range of lifesaving activities and is often attended by

CHALK AND CHEESE

In the Commonwealth some countries have wonderful facilities. In New Zealand the RLSS has access to jet-boats and a helicopter. But consider Barbados, with about half a million population. There is no swimming pool in Barbados, and all training and examinations are carried out in the open sea.

Heroic Rescue

1982: Kenneth John Raynor of Nottingham

A Water Spectacular was taking place at Colwick Country Park and members of the RLSS Lifeguard Club at the Park were engaged in ensuring the safety of the many participants; swimming in that portion of the West Lake normally set aside for this purpose should not have been taking place because the lifeguard patrol flags were not being flown. Although it was clear that they were behaving irresponsibly some 50 people were in the water. Three swam over to the booms that cordon off this area and one, Declan Quigley, who was a weak swimmer, lost his hold on the boom as he made his way along them with his companions. Within seconds, he disappeared from sight under the water. Members of the public summoned the Colwick Park Lifeguard Club patrol boat, *Errill P*, and other land-based lifeguards from the club to the scene. At once, a regular pattern of diving and searching was commenced by the lifeguards in the very murky waters around the boom from which Quigley had slipped. This was complemented by a line and anchor drag search, co-ordinated from the patrol boat. Kenneth Raynor completed ten free dives after swimming some 60yd to the scene, as a part of this search procedure. When the anchor caught on a submerged object, he then swam down the line to recover the casualty from the muddy bottom at a depth of some 20ft. With the assistance of Lifeguard David Morton, resuscitation was applied in the water until the casualty could be transferred to the patrol boat. Raynor continued resuscitation in the boat during the short trip to the bank. Despite all efforts at cardiopulmonary resuscitation by the lifeguards and by the ambulance crew, Declan Quigley was pronounced dead on arrival at hospital.

RLSS
LIFEGUARD

colleagues from Commonwealth branches. The summer schools attract men and women from not only Britain but the Cayman Islands, Kenya, Zambia, Australia, Canada, Cyprus, Hong Kong, Malaysia, Singapore, Sri Lanka, St Lucia, Tanzania, and Trinidad and Tobago. Many would not be able to be present but for the generous Laerdal scholarship and fellowship programmes. Of course, other branches run similar schemes. RLSS New Zealand held its first annual summer school in 1987. RLSS Canada has an annual symposium, providing discussion and debate for administrators, lifeguards, teachers, and researchers — all who are in any way involved in lifesaving and associated subjects.

Everywhere there was progress, confirmed by the Commonwealth Conferences of 1981 and 1986, though there was some concern that applications for the Mountbatten Medal were on the decrease. It was hoped that by circularising all the branches throughout the Commonwealth this could be remedied, for it was evident that some branch members were unaware of the existence of the medal. The 1986 Commonwealth Conference endorsed a proposal to create a Commonwealth Secretariat and appoint a Chief Secretary independent of RLSS UK. Since the Supplemental Charter of 1960, the Society's Chief Secretary had also been the Director of RLSS UK, and this dual role continued until 1986 when proposals on forward plan, sponsorship and regional development sprang from the knowledge that, with the unreserved

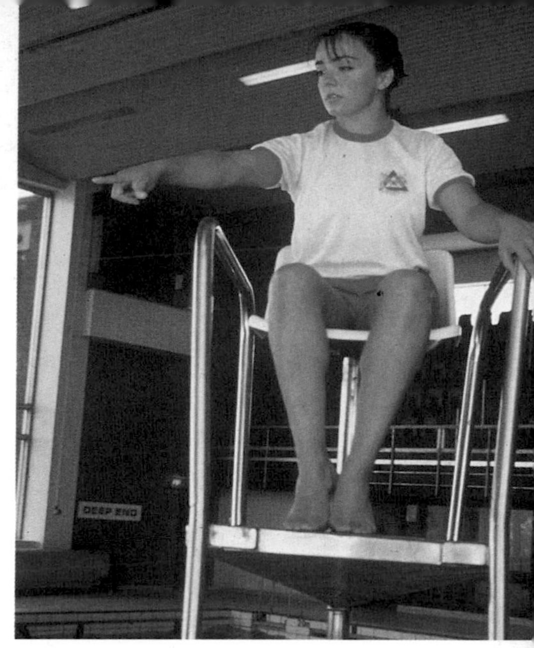

Above: There are no less than 1,900 teaching centres and 3,000 examiners in the UK

Opposite: A comforting sight for trainee swimmers, a lifeguard in the traditional red and yellow outfit

Below: Aquapack, the first UK water-safety package

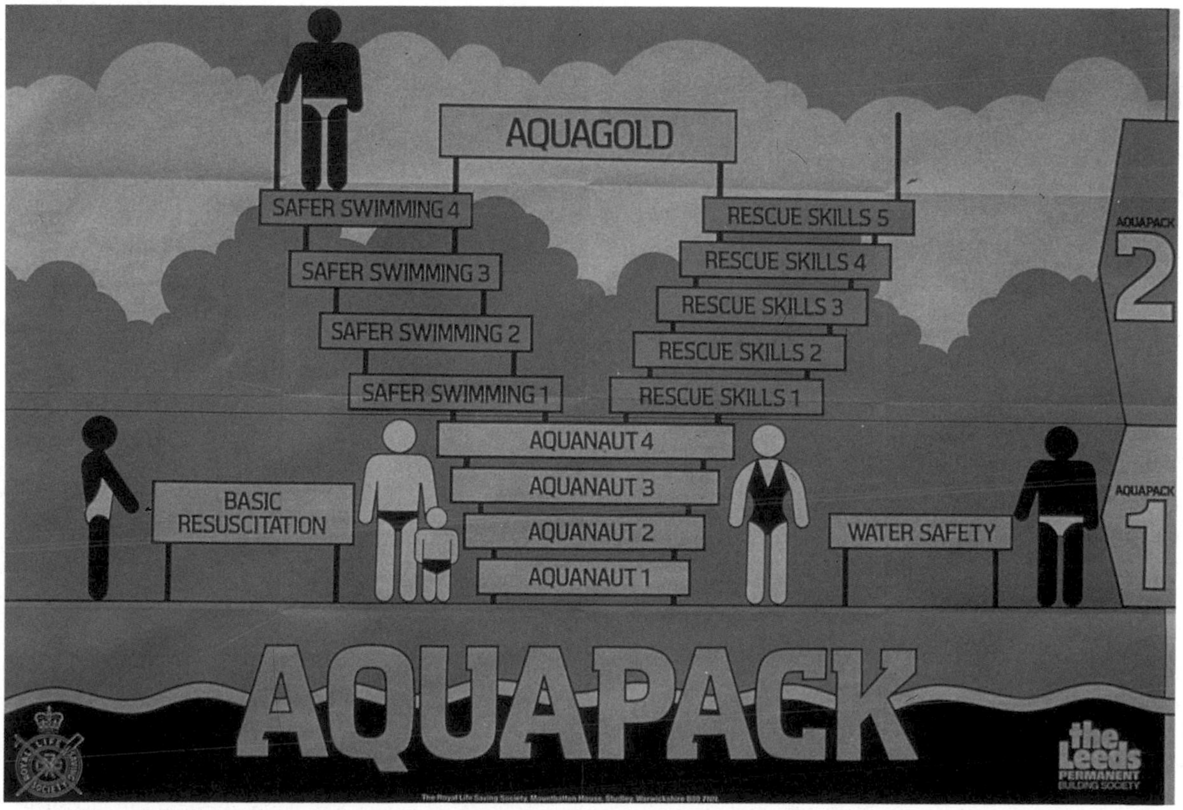

Without the dedicated work of the RLSS how many more people would die from drowning?

support of Member Branches, someone was available — the Chief Secretary — to take plans and principles forward.

Rescue 86 promised to be the largest ever gathering of lifesaving and lifeguarding personnel from around the world. It was organised by RLSS Canada for the WLS, and though not strictly a society event it paved the way for future events, such as Rescue 88 in Australia and Rescue 90 in Germany, proof, if any is needed, that lifesaving is a world issue. The location of Rescue 86 was Vancouver, Canada, and the event was an integral part of Expo 86.

An important step in lifesaving in Africa was taken in 1987 when a Lifesaving Workshop was established at the University of Zimbabwe, with delegates from ten African countries. This emphasises the deep commitment which the RLSS has always had to regional development, especially when this is linked to Third World countries.

Throughout the decade RLSS became better known; no longer was it associated in the public mind with lifeboats, but as with all voluntary organisations it needed to keep its image spick and span, to attract patronage and volunteers. Without volunteers the RLSS would cease to exist, and all were aware that the society was in direct competition with many others. Competitive events always attract volunteers, and the RLSS has more than most. One of the society's largest championships, the UK Lifesaving Championship, drew a total of more than 1,500 entrants in 1987, and was battled out at three levels — branch, region, and national. In the UK National Lifeguard Championship there were fifty-one teams.

After a visit from members of RLSS Australia to Britain in 1988 there was a UK tour of New Zealand and Australia to take part in the Asia Pacific Championships in Auckland and other events in Australia, and seventy-two competitors from 13 to 42 years throughout Britain applied for team selection. The final team comprised five men and five women, with two non-travelling reserves. Although the UK team headed the points table, it was not allowed to take the trophy as it was an invitation team only.

As the 1980s drew towards a close, no one could fail to marvel at the transformation of a society from a small group of dedicated and altruistic swimmers to an international organisation. In Britain in 1988 a total of 198,911 awards were achieved, including 120,839 Aquapack. Aquapack has been sponsored by Eurocamp, specialists in family holidays, since October 1988.

RLSS UK has 52 constituted branches, divided into 13 regions, and within these regions 140 Lifeguard units patrol pools, inland and coastal waters. There are no less than 1,900 teaching centres, and there is a force of more than 3,000 examiners. About half a million children and adults participate in some way in the work of the RLSS UK each year. These are daunting statistics. And so are those relating to Commonwealth branches; in Australia, with a population of 17 million, there are no less than 10,000 examiners.

Looking at the 1980s as a whole, one of the most exciting activities in the decade was the launch of Commonwealth Lifesaving Development Project, sponsored by Laerdal, which is a simple distance-learning package provided free to developing countries, and is a great success, with the pack included in many national school curricula. Informing and teaching the unknowing and the vulnerable remains a priority for the RLSS worldwide.

In 1987 in the UK 571 people died from accidental drowning, the third year in succession that fatalities by drowning, the third most common cause of accidental death, had decreased. This was despite the greatly increased use of water in all kinds of leisure activities, from the toddler in the tiny plastic-lined pool in the garden to the jet-skier. Without the dedicated work of the RLSS, what would the figure be? No one knows. No one will ever know.

The Thames Rescue Service is one of the busiest branches of the RLSS UK. What better advertisement for the RLSS than a spick and span boat

The Story of Resuscitation

Resuscitation techniques were known to the ancient Egyptians about 1300BC. There is a wall-painting relating to the attempt to resuscitate the King of Aleppo. Two attendants are turning him upside down. This method continued to to be practised until recent times, for resuscitation techniques have been determined more by chance than common sense. When the physiology of man was not understood, the most outlandish schemes were devised for restoring the apparently drowned to life.

Sometimes when a person was injured the right thing was done instinctively. When a bone was broken a splint made of bark was applied and examples of such splints date back as early as 2400BC. Bleeding from wounds was stopped by plugging, keeping the injured part cool, and elevating the limb, a method still used. The plugging employed was fresh meat, under the belief that this helped the healing process. Verdigris was used as a healing agent (and still is in France). Egyptian doctors also used two invaluable techniques for closing wounds — suturing (stitching) and taping.

Although it was discovered in ancient times that the heart was a pump, the interior of the body was very much of a mystery, and remained so until William Harvey (1578-1657) discovered the circulation of the blood, which in turn opened up the possibilities of understanding the respiratory processes. This of course is essential for any satisfactory resuscitation method. Many people disputed Harvey's claim, and a Mr Quekett said that Harvey never *saw* the circulation of the blood, and the first person who did was William Molyneux in 1683, and then it was in a newt.

Robert Hooke (1635-1703), a 'natural philosopher', as well as a Professor of Geometry, decided that 'breathing must be useful as it brings air into the lungs.' Ultimately resuscitation depends on keeping the heart and lungs working, and there were a variety of ways of accomplishing or trying to accomplish these tasks, some of them bizarre, some of them anticipating those of today.

JUST CAN'T HELP IT

I was called to examine a group of young lads for a resuscitation award. Somehow you know with the first few questions if you are going to have problems! 'Tell me why we breathe?' I asked. After a bit of deep breathing, breath holding, and looking very red in the face one boy answered 'Cos I can't help it!'

Frances Gerrard

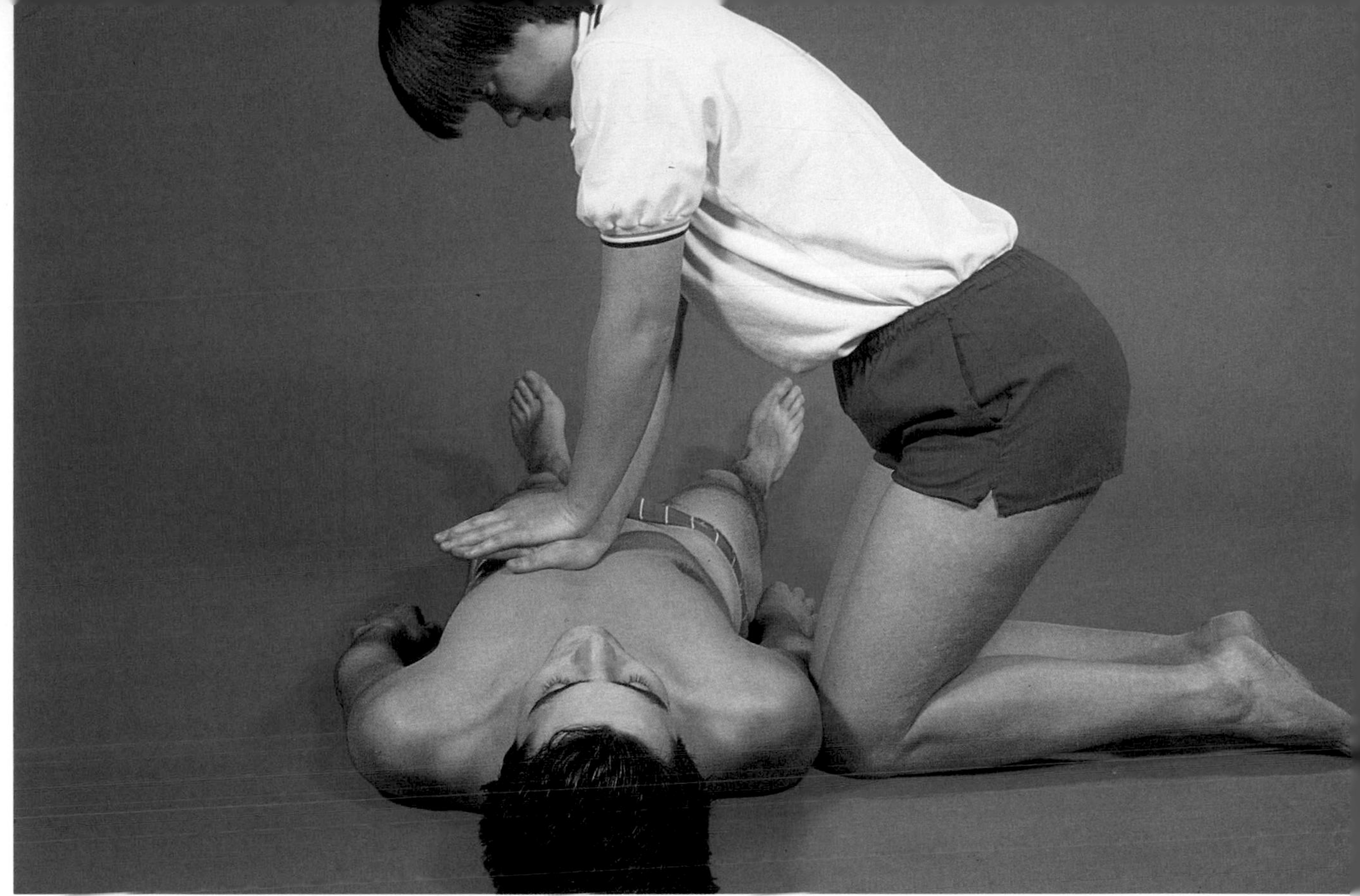

Compression to aid recovery, a far cry from the 1650 resuscitation when a 'lusty fellow' stamped upon a woman's breast and stomach to bring her back to life

As with external injuries, sometimes the best procedures were adopted without scientific or indeed any other kind of knowledge. For example, the modern method of mouth-to-mouth ventilation seems to be referred to in the Bible (II Kings, Chapter 4):

'And he went up and lay upon the child, and put his mouth upon his mouth, and his eyes upon his eyes: and he stretched himself upon the child: and the flesh of the child waxed warm.'

However, the best way of resuscitation, and a system that was employed throughout the known world irrespective of race or culture, was considered to be the infliction of pain. One means was flagellation, meant to arouse the victim from the deep sleep in which he or she had fallen, and any object that was handy could be used, although stinging nettles were favoured. This method has persisted into more sophisticated times, with wet cloths the preferred instrument.

As the body of a near victim of drowning was cold it seemed a good idea to warm it up to help revive him or her. Various items were placed on the casualty's stomach; these included ashes from a fire, hot water, and the dried excreta from domestic animals.

A curious method of resuscitation was practised by Byzantine doctors in the fourth century AD. This involved tossing the casualty in a blanket. Of far more significance was the idea of blowing air into the lungs; the alchemist and physician Paracelsus suggesting about 1530 that this should be done with a pair of bellows. This method was generally adopted, along with turning

A GOOD YEAR

One of the most active of branches in the UK is the Gosport and Fareham Inshore Rescue Service. A typical strenuous year was 1984 when members attended 148 separate incidents.

the victim upside down as practised by the ancient Egyptians. However, more strenuous methods were adopted by some.

In 1650 a woman who murdered her new-born child was hanged. She was put in a coffin, but bystanders heard a 'rattle in the throat.' One 'lusty fellow standing by stampt upon her breast and stomach severall tymes with his foot' while she was still in the coffin. This did not work so her blood was let, she was rubbed 'in severall places', and her throat was tickled with a feather. Amazingly she recovered and, because the new-born child had been stillborn and malformed, the conviction was reversed.

Transfusion of blood was regarded as a possible resuscitation technique, though no one knows why. It is believed that the first attempt was made on Pope Innocent VIII in 1492. It didn't work. In 1664 a Frenchman tried again, using lamb's blood. That didn't work either. The first successful transfusion between humans was in 1829, but the technique was always hazardous until 1900 when blood groups were discovered.

The Indians of North America resuscitated the apparently dead by puffing tobacco fumes into the lungs and rectum, and this was taken up by the whites about 1711 and was used for many years, being introduced into Europe in 1767. Because it was widely used in Holland, it was known as Dutch fumigation and was one of the favoured methods of the Royal Humane Society. In Australia casualties were 'smoked' over a fire.

Rolling an apparently drowned person on a barrel was often used, but the Swiss went one better in the eighteenth century by putting the casualty inside a barrel, which was then rotated. The idea behind this was to displace the stomach, which would put pressure on and off the chest as, presumably, the stomach bumped around. A severe jarring was also evident in the trotting horse

Heroic Rescue

1985: Holly Jacqueline Phillips of Richmond, Surrey

Holly Jacqueline Phillips (aged 15) was taking part in the Regatta festivities at Swanage Bay, Dorset in good weather with calm seas, when the ten-foot dinghy carrying her and Stephen Mundy (aged 18) capsized just off the stone quay. The boat was swept away on the very strong outgoing tide. Stephen swam after it but at approximately one hundred yards distance from the quay he became exhausted. Noticing his difficulties, Holly swam quickly to the rescue and upon reaching the casualty she found him to be semi-conscious and struggling feebly to grasp the mooring line of the boat. He was wearing overalls and heavy boots which the rescuer desperately tried to remove. Unable to accomplish this she immediately began a tow back to the shore reassuring the casualty in an attempt to make him relax. Half way to the shore the casualty lost consciousness but did not stop breathing; a boat came to assist but it proved impossible to lift Stephen's heavy and stiff body aboard and Holly continued with the tow checking at regular intervals that the casualty was breathing. A lifeboatman and fisherman assisted in lifting Stephen's body to the beach and he was placed in the recovery position until an ambulance took him to hospital.

St Paul's Churchyard where the Humane Society was founded in 1774

method, in which the dead rider bounced up and down on the horse's back.

Although Russia had formed a resuscitation society in St Petersburg the same year the Humane Society was formed, the peasants hundreds of miles away from modern sophistication had their own individual method, which was to put the casualty feet-first into a hole up to his or her chest. The hole was then partially filled in and the part of the head and body above ground was splashed with cold water. As with many techniques such as flagellation and electricity this relied upon shock. This and the trotting horse methods persisted into the nineteenth century.

One of the first recorded cases of resuscitating the apparently drowned is mentioned in the notes to William Derham's *Physico-Theology* as having occurred about 1650. In 1745 Dr J. Fothergill read a paper on the subject to the Royal Society. In 1767 several cases of resuscitation were reported in Switzerland, and a society was formed in Amsterdam to revive the apparently drowned and offer instruction to the ordinary people on the subject. In 1773 Dr A. Johnson suggested the formation of a similar society in England, and Dr William Hawes tried to form one, but there was a strong prejudice against this. However, he offered rewards to anyone who would rescue people from the Thames between Westminster and London Bridge and bring them to certain places on shore where, hopefully, they could be resuscitated.

He was personally instrumental in saving several lives, and paid the rewards out of his own money. His zeal was commended by all, and was one factor that led to the Humane Society (later Royal Humane Society) being founded in 1774.

Some time before 1744 a miner was resuscitated using the mouth-to-mouth method. Suitable candidates for this method, it was reckoned, would be those struck dead by lightning or by a

GHOSTS AND THINGS THAT GO SPLASH IN THE NIGHT

In China the spirit of a drowned man was said to wander over the water until appeased by the death of another person. In Germany all accidental drownings were due to the malignancy of the river spirit. Some people, if they saw a drowning, helped to finish the job off rather than try to rescue. And this is not in the distant past, but only about eighty years ago.

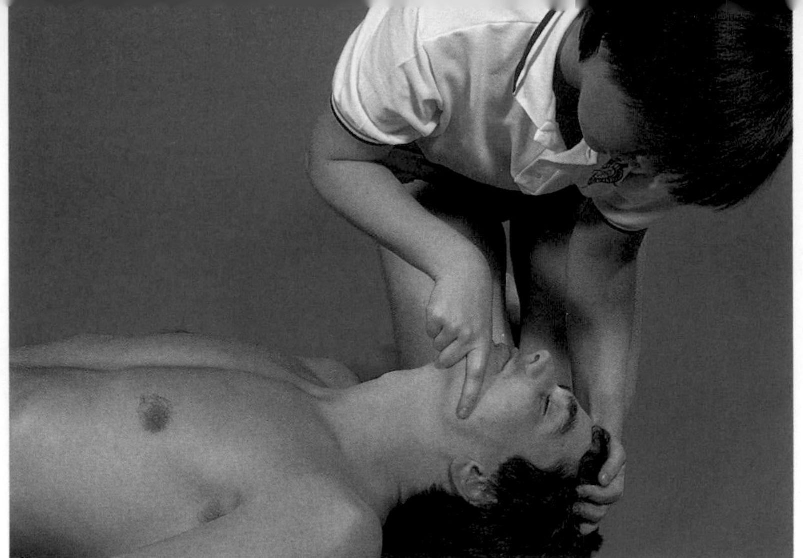

Positioning the 'casualty' for EAR resuscitation

> **MANIKINS**
>
> In 1960 a Norwegian toy maker showed the first manikin for teaching mouth-to-mouth resuscitation. The result was Resusci Anne, used by millions. But not in water. So Resusci Junior was introduced, a 'boy' of five who would sink to the bottom of the pool or float. These have been followed by Recording Resusci Anne, Resusci Junior, and Skillmeter Resusci Anne that incorporates sensors for assessing responsiveness, opening the airway and checking a pulse, with a liquid crystal display monitor that records the assessment sequence and compressions and ventilations by means of moving bars. A printer can produce a read-out.

sudden fit of passion. Unfortunately not many people are around when someone is struck dead by lightning or dies of a sudden fit of passion (except in films or on television), and surgeons looked around for the newly departed to practise on. It was suggested that 'malefactors executed at the gallows would afford opportunities for discovering how far this method might be successful'. One of these experiments was carried out on Dr Dodd, who was hanged for forgery at Tyburn in 1777. What gives this case particularly poignancy was that Dr Dodd had been Governor of the Humane Society. For those who like extra details, Dr Dodd forged a bond for £4,200 signed Lord Chesterfield. And the attempted resuscitation failed.

However, there were successes, improbable as it may seem, though how far these can be authenticated is a moot point, for, as in Dr Johnson's published case histories, with a limited amount of data available it is tempting to opt for hearsay evidence. Johnson quoted the case of Patrick Redmond, hanged for robbery. Dr Dodd had been strung up for an hour before being cut down, and Redmond twenty-nine minutes. Redmond's veins were opened, and it was observed, not surprisingly, that circulation had ceased. For four hours his neck, mouth and back were rubbed with oils and spirits, and then the 'corpse' was subjected to infusions of tobacco fumes. An incision was then made in the trachea (windpipe) and a cannula (surgical tube) was inserted, through which air was blown. After twenty minutes blood began to flow from the incision, and after a time the pulse returned. Five hours had passed since the hanging.

When the Humane Society was formed it disowned the resuscitation methods involving turning the individual upside down or placing round, in, or under a barrel. That the barrel method continued to be popular amongst the peasantry is evident from the fact that the society continued to publish condemnation of the barrel method right up to 1909.

The importance of the Humane Society can hardly be overemphasised, and it was a direct forerunner of the Royal Life Saving

Society. Its purpose was 'for affording immediate relief to persons apparently dead from drowning', and its motto was *Latiat scintillula forsan* ('a small spark may perhaps lie hid'). Its founder members were Drs Goldsmith (better known as a poet and playwright, author of *She Stoops to Conquer)*, Heberden, Towers, Lettsom, Hawes — of course — and Cogan, but predominantly the last three.

The inaugural meeting was held in the Chapter Coffee House in St Paul's Churchyard where Drs Hawes and Cogan had invited thirty-two prominent men. Societies for getting information to the public on resuscitating the drowned had been started throughout Europe. It was a facet of the Age of Reason. Why let people die when there was no reason for it? The same process can be seen in midwifery, and the foundation of lying-in hospitals and orphanages; the first kept the children alive and the second kept them from being thrown on the human scrap-heap.

The members of the Humane Society were not hidebound; they were open to suggestions, and in 1776 Dr Hawes approached the celebrated doctors Hunter and Cullen for their help in selecting the best and safest method of reviving a drowned person, bearing in mind that the ordinary man in the street might be called upon to act as rescuer and that complicated apparatus was unlikely to be available. This cut out immediately the possibility that the new wonder of the age, electricity, might be suitable for the masses.

Electricity was a fashionable hobby. Louis XV had witnessed the administration of an electric shock to a line of monks a mile long, and when they all jumped in the air he was convulsed with

TAKE YOUR CHOICE

A strange word, manikin. It can mean the same as mannequin. it can mean a dwarf. Or, in its better-known usage, an anatomical model. It comes from the Dutch word meaning man. For those not very good at spelling, manikin has the advantage of being also mannikin and manakin. Take your choice.

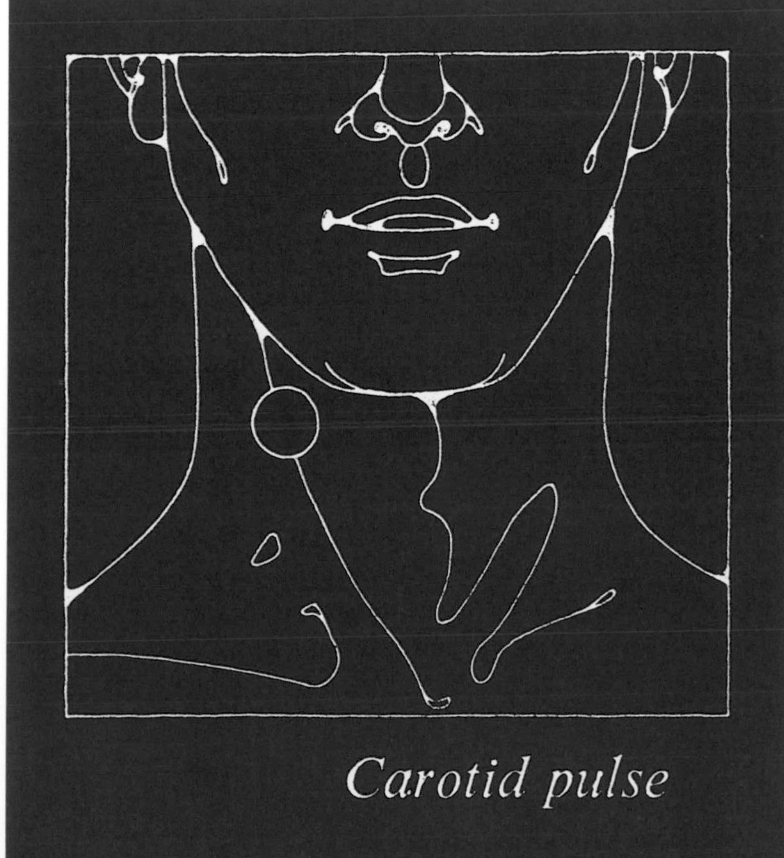

A graphic explanation of where the carotid pulse is, far more reliable a guide than the wrist

laughter. Public demonstrations of the powers and potential of electricity were greeted with awe, and one of the set pieces was a glass of brandy ignited by a spark shooting from the end of a man's finger. The founder of Methodism, John Wesley, became a firm believer in the curative powers of electricity for a wide range of diseases from malaria to hysteria, and fervently advocated intense and lengthy electric shocks.

In 1748 the American president Benjamin Franklin, who was also one of the great inventors of the age and who had provided Buckingham Palace with a lightning conductor as soon as George III had bought the building, had, at a picnic, 'killed a turkey by the electric spark, and roasted it by an electric jack before a fire kindled by an electric bottle.' Cases of resuscitation by electricity, true or fanciful, were duly logged with the Humane Society, though because electricity was a mystery it could be a dangerous process, and several persons were killed whilst experimenting. However, it is worth mentioning that, within a quarter of a century of the formation of the Humane Society, Humphry Davy had produced electric light with carbon points.

A CORNISH WAVE

'I was not sure if she was in trouble but then she screamed for help and started waving her hands about. The stupid thing was that all the people on the cliffs started waving back, thinking she was just being friendly.'

Eyewitness at a near tragedy in North Cornwall in 1988

Electricity was therefore one more option for the Humane Society to consider. When asked by the society for recommendations, Dr Cullen made a list of procedures:

restoration of body heat
fumigation via the rectum
use of bellows to insufflate the lungs
venesection of the jugular vein
application of stimulants
the giving of emetics

John Hunter had been investigating resuscitation techniques for more than twenty years. He had ascertained that cardiac arrest always followed the cessation of breathing in asphyxia, and that distention of the lungs stimulated a reflex action that started the heart beating again. He emphasised the importance of filling the victim's lungs with air, and, a brilliant hypothesis, suggested the use of oxygen, only discovered by Joseph Priestley two years before. Second in importance was the application of warmth, but with discretion as it had been found that with frozen birds sudden heat had killed them outright. Thirdly, he advocated stimulants to the nose and throat, and also to the bowels by using an enema. He was decidedly against the fashionable use of fumigation by tobacco smoke, the forcing down of emetics, and bleeding.

Hunter had his priorities right. To put air into the lungs he recommended the use of a double-chamber bellows. And he also experimented with intravenous injections, though these did not seem to do any good. Mouth-to-mouth ventilation was not favoured.

Hunter's recommendations were widely taken up. He had

looked at all the alternatives and came up with a system that made sense, and his views on the efficacy of oxygen were regarded seriously. A good deal of research went into the construction of a suitable bellows, and in 1786 Charles Kite, a Gravesend surgeon, invented one that was taken up by the Humane Society — though on many occasions it was not resorted to, probably for the simple reason that there was not one available when a drowning or near-drowning occurred. Kite's bellows had valves, installed in such a way that both inflation and deflation of the lungs were possible.

Use of these bellows was a two-man effort. One of them placed the nozzle in one of the victim's nostrils; the other sealed the other nostril and held the mouth closed. The first man depressed the bellows, at the same time applying pressure on the larynx, stopping air entering the stomach. When the chest of the casualty expanded the thorax was depressed by applying pressure on the diaphragm. Kite also devised an electrical instrument, but was aware that this could be dangerous.:

> 'When I have electrified the body, all other operations have been suspended, lest the assistants should receive the shock instead of the patient; which may readily happen, as the living body is a much better conductor of the electric fluid than the dead.'

By shielding the electrodes, an electric shock could be given while the patient was in a warm bath 'or surrounded with hot grains'. However, Kite, despite his willingness to experiment, had doubts about the use of oxygen, also known as dephlogisticated air, considering it no better than ordinary air, and he continued to believe in the use of bleeding.

Kite's electrical apparatus was too large and cumbersome to be carried by individuals, and he co-operated with John Savigny, a maker of surgical equipment, to produce a more portable version.

Despite the existence of the Humane Society, it was felt that many, both doctors and the general public, remained in ignorance of advancing resuscitation technology, and even those who knew about it had no idea of priorities or remained committed to early obsolescent procedures. Medical men in general practice preferred old and trusted methods, even if not particularly effective, well into the nineteenth century. A typical example was the refusal on the part of many to use the stethoscope. A firm list of priorities was laid down in Denmark by J. D. Herboldt and C.G. Rafn.

(1) remove anything restricting the natural functioning of the body
(2) restore the function of respiration
(3) restore the function of circulation
(4) restore the function of 'the suppressed energy of the nerves'

OFF THE MARK

A few years ago I was judging a staged incident competition, and by chance was sitting next to the pool manager (Banbury Outdoor Pool). A fully clothed woman 'fell' into the water and screamed for help. The rescuers were slow off the mark, the screams were very realistic, the pool manager (Wally) was so well trained that by the fourth or fifth scream he could bear it no longer and dived in to perform a rescue, fully clothed and with his cigarette still in his mouth. We were absolutely stunned, and then proud on two counts. One — the scenario was as real as it could be, and, two — the pool staff were so highly trained they could not ignore the screams for help. You can imagine the applause from the spectators, who were probably unaware of the full situation, and why Wally's face was so red. Judgment as to his technique and quickness of action came in the local hostelry later that evening.

A small tale but one I think with a message. If one is a highly trained lifesaver and one sees somebody struggling and screaming for help, even if your conscious knows it is a fake the subconscious can send one into action — better to be safe than sorry.

Alan Asquith

'The insufflation of air by the mouth is a very toilsome and loathsome act'

Of particular interest is their advocacy of mouth-to-mouth ventilation, resulting in a predictable backlash, for the age was not only one of reason and scientific discovery but one of increasing delicacy. One anonymous reaction was typical of many in the same strain:

> 'the insufflation of air by the mouth is a very toilsome and loathsome act, and since accordingly an otherwise laudable delicacy of feeling usually prohibits both the Physician and other people of propriety from using this method, especially in adults or people of advanced years who have been drowned, it is only of little use.'

It is very evident that the complainant is a medical man, judging by the content and by the use of the work 'insufflation', a term not used by laymen.

In some quarters resuscitation was treated seriously, especially in lying-in hospitals, the product of enlightened midwifery. In 1802 successful resuscitation, mainly it is believed, mouth-to-mouth, was practised on 500 stillborn children, and the matron, Mrs Ann Newby, was rewarded by the Humane Society with their medal.

One of the more curious methods of resuscitation, which appears to have stood the test of time, was investigated in 1811 by Benjamin Brodie, a rising young surgeon of twenty-eight. In 1810 he had been made a Fellow of the Royal Society, and in the fullness of time was knighted for his services to medicine. This strange method was the old Red Indian method, fumigation, forcing tobacco fumes into the intestines through the rectum. Brodie discovered by experiments on animals that it was more likely to kill than cure. Notwithstanding his considered judgement, many continued to believe right through the nineteenth century that the introduction into the rectum of irritants worked, and the Royal Humane Society advocated the use of hartshorn (ammonia water) and mustard. In 1815 James Curry invented a surgical instrument for this very purpose, a kind of large syringe. One later writer described it as a forerunner of the grease gun.

FIGHTING TALK

'The old system of letting any swimmer act as drowning man is radically wrong because it leaves open the door to favouritism. In many such contests we have seen the supposed drowning man struggle violently with one competitor, while with another he has been eminently peaceable. It may not have been with the actual thought of destroying the first competitor's chances, but it has resulted in that, all the same.'

William Henry, 1893

Resuscitation became a subject for rising young stars in the medical firmament to investigate or pontificate upon. Astley Cooper is best known today for his invention of the Astley Cooper chair for children, an uncomfortable straight-backed chair that would prevent the young from sitting slovenly, but he was also willing to contribute to the resuscitation debate. His recommendations were sensible. He suggested that in manual ventilation the thorax and the abdomen should be compressed simultaneously. The air would thus be expelled, and the elastic recoil of the areas compressed would induce inhalation.

There were some techniques that could not be improved. They were basic and down to earth. But where there was general scientific progress and discovery there were always possibilities for resuscitationists. Advances in electricity followed one after the other; one of the consequences was the concept of the 'reanimation chair' using both electricity and bellows.

As in all spheres where there is enthusiasm there is euphoria. Benjamin Brodie added a note of unwanted pessimism. There were, he said, few cases of drowning in which artificial respiration would prove of any service. There was a time limit of three minutes from the cessation of breathing before the heart stopped, and this, said Brodie, was final. His judgement countered a good deal of the folk history of resuscitation. There were also stern words from a Paris doctor, Leroy d'Etiolles, who said that the uninstructed use of bellows could kill the casualty in a variety of ways, and this caused a good deal of worry amongst those who

There was, said Benjamin Brodie, a time limit of three minutes from the cessation of breath before the heart stopped. Speedy action was, and is vital

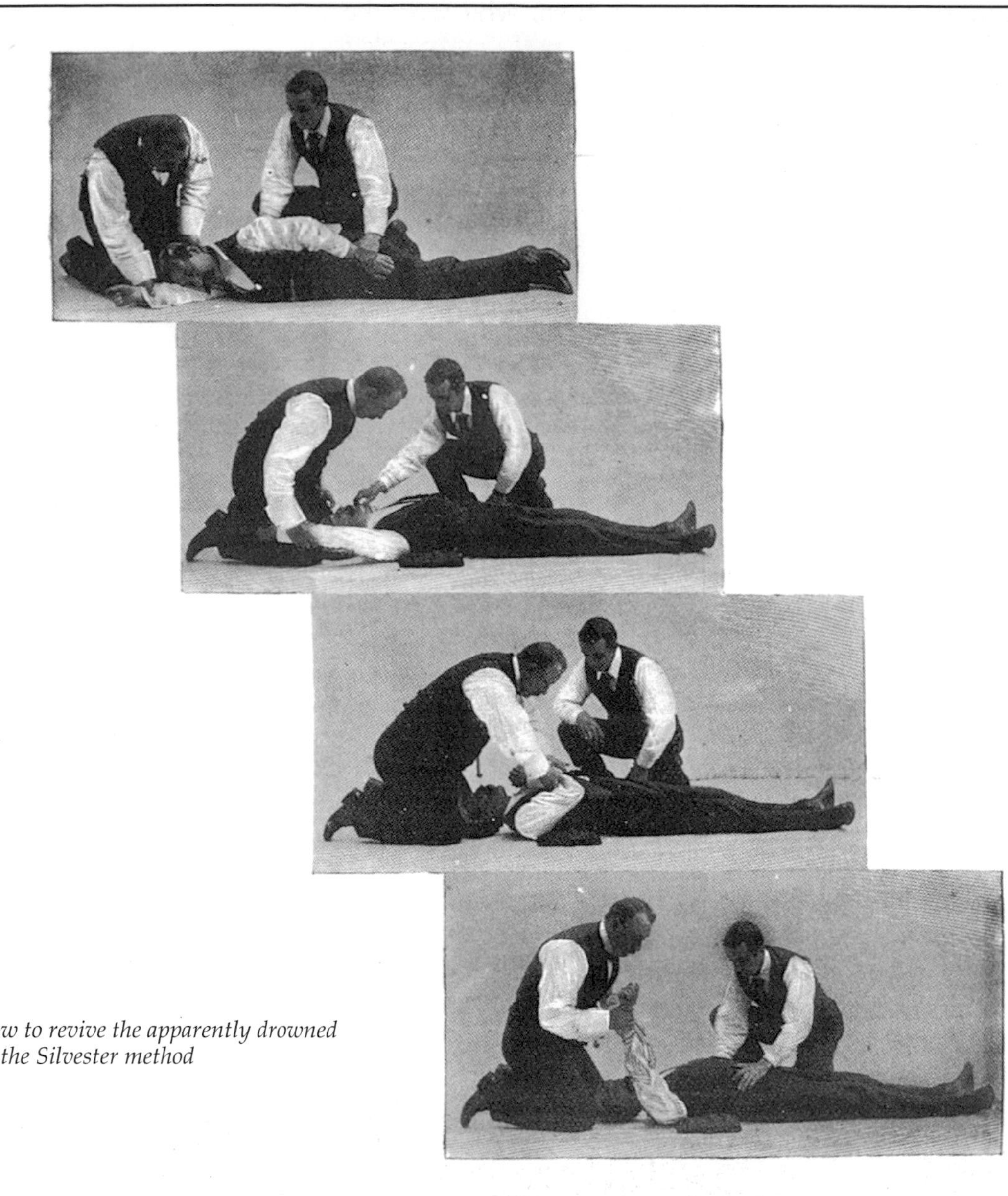

How to revive the apparently drowned by the Silvester method

continued to propagate this technique.

D'Etiolles favoured manual resuscitation, using the pressure of the hands to expel air and relying on the elasticity of the body to take in air. Gradually manual means gained favour, and there were variations, with a length of cloth wound under and over the body and an assistant at each end to compress the chest, release, and compress again. This method, evolved by John Dalrymple, was taken up by the Royal Humane Society in 1833 and was in favour, together with a variation in which the cloth was twisted, until the arrival of the better-known Silvester method.

The bellows method came and went in popularity, and research was undertaken into the kind of air that was best — cold air, warm air, oxygen, or a combination. John Erichsen, who won the Fothergill Medal of the Royal Humane Society in 1845, advocated an oxygen and tepid air mix, and devised an instrument to infuse this. Mouth-to-mouth resuscitation was still regarded with hostility because of its aesthetic inacceptibility, and the kind of mask used by anaesthetists was employed.

Some of the techniques were practised on corpses. There was always an ample supply of these, but any shortage was made up by the body snatchers and resurrectionists who disinterred newly buried bodies. Some of the body snatchers went too far, and killed to order. The two most famous were Burke and Hare (Burke was hanged in 1829, Hare, who had turned King's Evidence, lived until the 1860s). They killed by suffocation to leave no marks on the body, a form of murder that became known as burking.

From a series of experiments it was found that if a victim was placed on his or her back it was likely that the airway would be blocked by the tongue falling backwards. It is rather surprising that this was not discovered before (obviously it was, but the phenomenon had not been recorded). So the casualty was placed face downwards, so that the tongue fell forwards. Dr Marshall Hall (not to be confused with the barrister of the same name) developed what was perhaps the first systematic prone method of resuscitation.

The victim was placed face down with a pad beneath the chest. Pressure was applied by the operator to the thorax, causing expiration, and when this pressure was relaxed the victim was rolled, one hand under the shoulder, one hand on the hip, to cause inspiration. When the shoulder is moved in this situation, muscles become tense, and the thorax expands. It all seemed very straightforward and in 1856 Marshall Hall published his method. By the following year twenty-three persons had recovered from drowning by this system being used, but Marshall Hall died before he could refine and develop his method, and it was left to others to carry on his work, such as Rose and Silvester.

Silvester's method in a modified form is that used today by many lifesaving organisations, although Silvester adopted the face-up system, and so it was often advisable to have an assistant to hold the tongue clear. The main disadvantage of the Silvester method was that it was exceptionally tiring for all but the experienced practitioner, and many tried to make the practice easier for the untrained. Unquestionably there was still scope for variation; some were violent, some needed three operators, and some were complicated for the sake of being complicated.

However, the folk remedies, the inconsequential trial-and-error procedures, were to all intents and purposes exploded, though there was still more to find out. Medical science was advancing rapidly along with specialised surgical equipment. The science of microscopy was at a high level, and the introduction of the binocular microscope was a sterling help to doctors.

QUACK!

How many entertainments are practised in the water today? Certainly fewer than was the case a century ago when an endless supply of games and sports kept the swimmers and the spectators happy. The Water Derby featured men mounted on barrels fitted with horses' heads and labelled with the names of well-known racehorses. They were provided with paddles for the 'race.' At one time duck hunts were popular. A live duck was used, the swimmer first catching it taking the prize, but the threat of prosecution put an end to the use of a live duck. At a London gala one of the items on the programme was a duck hunt and in due course the SPCA (the forerunner of the RSPCA) turned up, only to find that the duck was in fact a human swimmer, recruited to act as target. Boxing and wrestling in water were also common, mounted wrestling, with one swimmer walking on the bottom and bearing the wrestler on his shoulders, being especially liked.

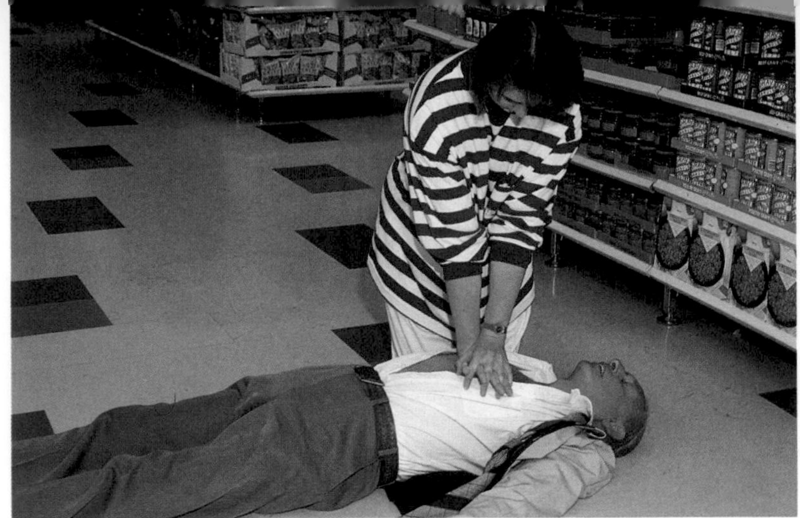

The need for quick positive resuscitation may occur anywhere, as for instance in this posed situation in a supermarket

Attention was turned to physiology. It had been believed that water did not enter the lungs during drowning, because no water had been found in the victims' lungs during the post mortem. This was untrue. Sometimes the water was absorbed into the system.

It was all very well making discoveries and offering recommendations, but learned papers are only read by learned people. When the St John Ambulance Association was formed in 1877, its first-aid handbook was a major contribution to the large scale promulgation of modern and unprejudiced resuscitation methods. And fourteen years later the Swimmers' Life-saving Society was formed, using the most efficient and up-to-date methods. Which, of course, the society as the RLSS has continued to do.

The introduction of oxygen cylinders was a valuable aid in

OH YES?

'It is a fact that bathing and the frequent wetting of the head causes scurf to accumulate, thereby creating baldness. In order to prevent this unwelcome state of affairs all swimmers should be advised in time and send for a bottle of 'Alexia' which is a delightful preparation for invigorating the hair and keeping the scalp in a healthy and clean condition.'

Advertisement in *Swimming*, 15 August 1895

Where necessary, manual methods of resuscitation are still used

resuscitation techniques, but their use rather depended on where the casualty was. And when a drowning occurred it was usually not within reach of oxygen apparatus. There was still some time to go before the unquestionably best method was accepted — mouth-to-mouth or mouth-to-nose.

The 'hammock' method announced in 1923 is a descendant of the Byzantine blanket technique, and as with the Swiss in-a-barrel method relied on displacing the internal organs to create expiration. And in the same year another old method was reintroduced under a new name — counter-shock; this was to resuscitate apparently dead people who had been electrocuted. The process was simple. The unfortunate casualty was dropped on the ground from the distance of a foot. It was soon realised that this was no way to deal with casualties.

Most 'new' techniques were variations of old ones, usually manual, and mainly involved changes of position, though the Holger Nielsen method of 1931 was superior to most and was adopted by many of the rescue agencies, including, for a time, the RLSS until 1965. It was originally a two-man method but in 1932 Nielsen converted it into a one-man system, far more useful for emergencies.

The operator set himself at the head of the prone casualty, kneeling or half-kneeling, with hands over the person's shoulder blades, rocking forward until his weight was over his hands. Pressure was kept for two seconds, then released. The operator slid his hands down the arms of the casualty to just above the

TOO CONVINCING

Personally my main memory of realistic lifesaving was at a police cadets' competition when I was an unconscious body. After I was landed, I heard the competitor ask the judge 'Is she breathing?'

'No,' the judge replied.

'Oh God!' said the police cadet, who then proceeded to give mouth to mouth resuscitation for real!'

Esme Wilson

Most new techniques were variations on old ones

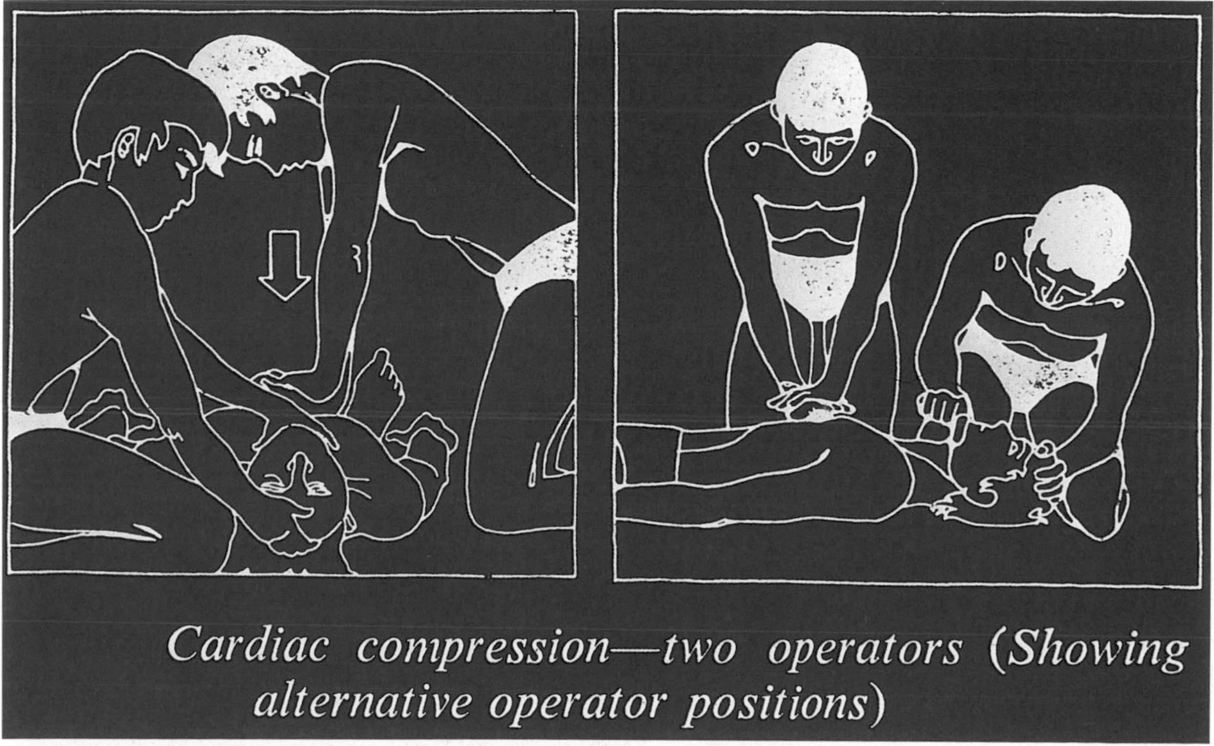

Cardiac compression—two operators (Showing alternative operator positions)

elbows. Arms were then raised to their full extent, and lowered (two seconds). The operator then returned his hands up the arms back to the shoulder blades and the cycle was repeated. Each cycle took six seconds, ten to the minute. Compared with some of the more exotic acrobatics involved in some techniques it was ridiculously simple, but it seemed to work, and it could be practised by those who had only recently been introduced to lifesaving techniques.

Early investigations into what were to become pacemakers were begun in the early 1930s, and this involved inserting a long needle through the chest wall into the heart and electrifying it so that the heart would be reactivated, but the success rate was less than 50 per cent and more sophisticated means had a long way to wait. Suction cups to the abdomen had been practised for some time, with handles that were raised and lowered.

Many of the manual techniques were developed under the assumption that the casualty would have a clear space around him or her so that the operator would have plenty of room, and a good deal of thought was applied to the case of the casualty who is trapped or in a constricted situation. Others were developed involving apparatus unlikely to be around, such as the rocking chair method; the operator sat in the rocking chair and, less shoes, used his feet to put pressure on the thorax of the casualty as he

One of the modern aids to acquiring resuscitation techniques. The air goes into the calibrated bag on the chest instead of the lungs

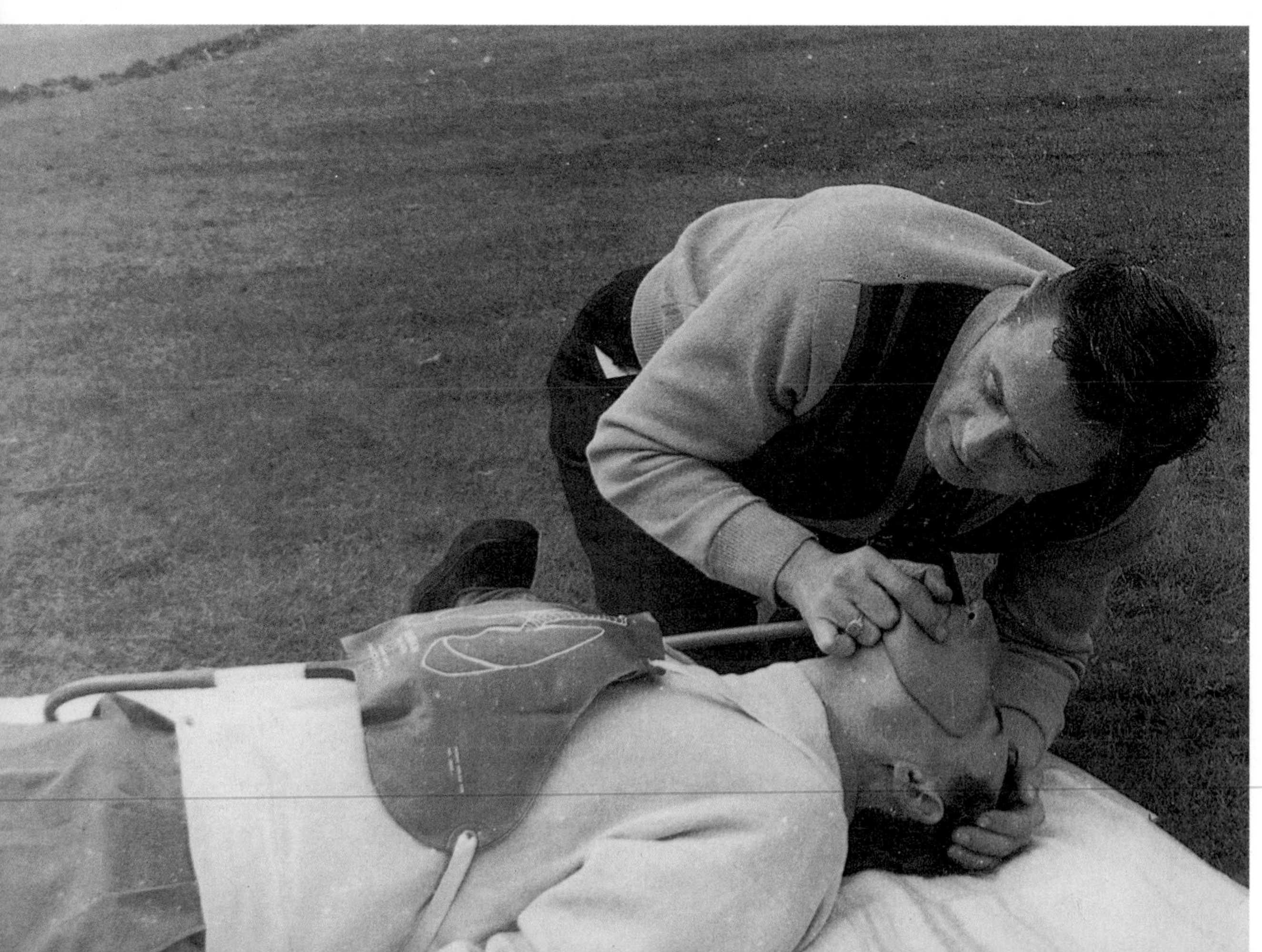

rocked back, releasing the pressure as he rocked forward, hoping that the recoil of the victim's chest would cause inspiration.

Some systems were more violent than others. The classic method was pounding on the victim's chest with a clenched fist. In a way, this harks back to the very early methods when a severe pummelling was thought to bring results. There was certainly no shortage of investigation into resuscitation, many of them developed by the United States military. A version of the now old-established Silvester method was adopted for a sitting casualty. Casualties in aircraft who could not be moved were responsible for many of these new techniques.

It is difficult to say when mouth-to-mouth ventilation became acceptable and rendered most other methods obsolete. Certainly it was discussed by the National Executive of the RLSS in 1959 and considered unpleasant and unsanitary, and the use of a plastic tube was marketed commercially to assuage disgust. Many thought that aesthetic objections to the expired air (mouth-to-mouth) technique were pathetic when someone's life was at stake, but this is not the first time delicacy has been put before efficiency, and certainly not the last. It is interesting to puzzle out how the authorities of the 1950s would have dealt with an advertising campaign telling of the dangers of AIDS.

A girl demonstrating the recovery position

The Commonwealth Conference of the RLSS held during July 1961 reversed the decision made two years earlier regarding the expired air method, though terms of reference had to be sorted out. Canada was using the term 'Rescue Breathing', while Australia and New Zealand went along with the British definition. It is significant that the 'questions of race, religion and colour had to be taken into practical consideration'. The National Executive in the UK declared that each branch should have the use of a full-size manikin, and a film or film-loop with the necessary projection equipment. Smaller branches needed to make arrangements with organisations such as the St John Ambulance Brigade, the Police, the Fire Service, and the Red Cross to share facilities.

The advantages of the expired air method (known as EAR) were definitively set out, and there was no argument:

(1) it can be started at an early stage.
(2) it provides a greater exchange of gases than manual methods
(3) no equipment is needed
(4) both the operator's hands are free to ensure the airway is free
(5) it is not tiring to the operator.

As more investigation was carried out, it became evident that mouth-to-nose resuscitation was advisable as there was less chance of the air entering into the stomach

It says a great deal for the RLSS that immediately it had made its decision to adopt the expired air system it did the utmost to publicise the method to the general public with books, pamphlets, leaflets, and demonstrations, with an emphasis on inculcating children, the lifesavers and rescuers of the future.

Theory is one thing. Practice is another. The expired air method works, and it has saved thousands of lives. And no doubt those who have practised on a manikin have confidence in their abilities. And that applies too to manual methods. But here is a most graphic account of an incident that occurred a few years ago. The narrator is Frank Mortimer and the account was published in the newsletter of the Suffolk branch:

> My two sons (then age 14 years and 16 years) were picnicing on the banks of the Thames at Windsor when Ian, the younger, spotted a middle-aged lady apparently in difficulty in the middle of the river. He approached the family on the bank and was assured that she was a strong swimmer and was all right. When they looked again the lady had disappeared. I made a note of my boys' comments afterwards at the Police Station.
>
> 'It's cold, dark and lonely searching the bottom under 12 feet of water.'
>
> 'I found the body but my lungs were bursting and there were spots before my eyes. I had to surface before I passed out.'
>
> 'My greatest fear when I went down again was what would happen if she recovered and grabbed me.'
>
> 'It's different doing resuscitation kneeling in mud and shivering so much I could hardly breathe.'
>
> 'The woman was sick twice and so was I.'
>
> 'The smell was terrible. I took off my T-shirt and wiped her face, she stopped breathing again and I knew I had to carry on. I was sick again.'
>
> 'It was such a shock to find no pulse, her eyes were dilated — God, her heart's stopped.'
>
> 'After a few compressions, the pulse started again. I felt like crying.'
>
> 'A man pushed me out of the way and started mouth-to-mouth but I could see he didn't know what he was doing. I tried to tell him but he wouldn't listen.'
>
> 'I didn't sleep last night. I kept thinking about it and feeling sick.'
>
> 'It was so different, so very different, from our nice warm swimming pool.'
>
> Unfortunately the casualty, a lady doctor, died in the ambulance on the way to the hospital.
>
> Both boys were awarded the Royal Humane Society Award.

A NATIONAL AWARD

In 1988 two women lifeguards who saved a three-year-old girl from drowning in a Midland swimming pool were recommended for national awards by Birmingham City Council. The girl was in the shallow end of the pool when her rubber ring upended, trapping her underwater. Her father pulled her out and the lifeguards gave her artificial respiration for several minutes before the victim began to breathe again. 'The little girl had swallowed a lot of water', said the pool manager, 'and had swallowed her own tongue. My staff did very well, they stayed calm and did not panic.'

To the author's mind this is the most graphic description of being at the sharp end of lifesaving that he has ever read. It should be compulsory reading.in every manual on lifesaving.

Giving mouth to mouth resuscitation immediately, thus saving valuable time

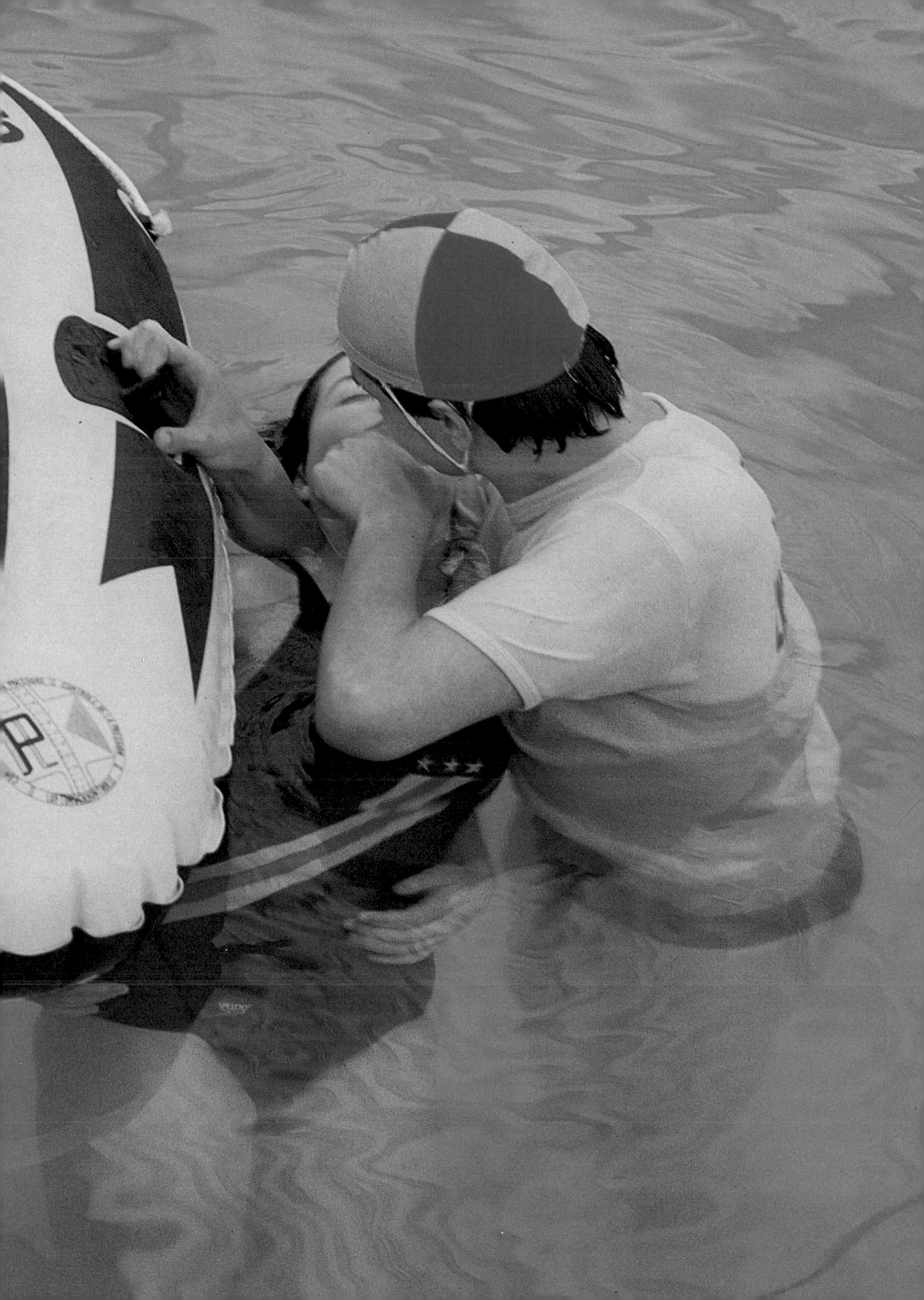

The History of Swimming

'The ability to save life is the glorious privilege of a swimmer, and many are ever ready to risk their own lives in order to aid others in danger'

Swimming (1893) by Archibald Sinclair and William Henry

Without the ability to swim there would be no lifesavers. Swimming represents the victory of the human race over an alien environment. It is the most powerful weapon in the armoury of the lifesaver, and its importance cannot be overestimated.

No one knows when man first discovered that he could swim, although there is sculpture from the ancient city of Nineveh, some now in the British Museum, dating from about 880-650BC depicting Assyrians of the time swimming in various ways, especially the front crawl, often assisted by an inflated animal skin known as a mussuk. There were races in Japan in 36BC, and the Japanese were the first to organise swimming on a national basis. An imperial edict in 1603 made swimming compulsory in schools, and a three-day swimming meeting was set up as early as 1810. As Japan was closed to the western nations, nothing was known of this.

In civilisations that had not mastered the art of bridge-building, swimming was often necessary to cross rivers, but it was in the military field that swimming was most essential, and there are many references in Roman history and literature to swimming. Julius Caesar is reported to have saved his life many times by swimming from a sinking ship. Roman youths training for a military career swam in the River Tiber running by the Campus Martius, and the therapeutic value of swimming was evident — there were alleged to be 850 public baths in ancient Rome, all with provision for swimming. The ability to swim was rated highly; an ignorant man, according to a Roman proverb, was someone 'who neither knows how to read or to swim.'

Greek legend has its swimmers, in particular Leander, who

TRAVELLING IN STYLE

Although a poor swimmer, Chief Petty Officer John Payne went to the rescue of a drowning pensioner off Gibraltar in 1988, and although battered by a six-foot wave into an underwater cave and stung by sea eggs — poisonous sea anemones — he not only managed to save the man, but also the lives of two others who had gone in to help in the rescue. Although exhausted, there was no room for him in the ambulance and he was obliged to travel to hospital in a hotel garbage truck.

The Serpentine was perhaps the most popular swimming place in Britain in the late nineteenth century. On warm days there could be 1,200 swimmers

was in love with a priestess, Hero, and who at night swam the Hellespont (the Dardanelles between European and Asiatic Turkey) to be with her, guided by a lighted torch she held. Eventually he made the trip once too often, and drowned. The poet Lord Byron did the same thing and survived to tell the tale (many times). There is a graphic description of Leander's feat in 'Hero and Leander', a poem by Thomas Hood (1799-1845):

> His eyes are blinded with the sleety brine,
> His ears are deafened with the wildering noise;
> He asks the purpose of her fell design,
> But foamy waves choke up his struggling voice.
> Under the ponderous seas his body dips,
> And Hero's name dies bubbling on his lips.

There are many accounts of swimming throughout history. Charlemagne (742-814) was said to be one of the best swimmers of his day, and Louis XI and his courtiers are known to have swam in the Seine. Some of the claims arouse a degree of scepticism. The Vikings, it is said, 'could swim in armour and dive and take it off under water, so as to elude an enemy.'

There must have been instruction in swimming, though little is

The 'natural' swimming stroke, described as early as 1587

Opposite : Swimming competitions in the early years were often replete with tricks and gimmicks as in this 1872 coloured print. One dreads to think what is going to happen next

recorded and in the *Quarterly Review* of June 1826 James Skene wrote that 'we shall in vain search our libraries for one tolerably useful and practical treatise on the art of swimming' but he was in error, for there had been previous publications. Techniques were rough and ready, though the dog paddle and a method akin to the crawl stroke were being supplemented. The frog was set up as an example of efficient natural swimming, and the *Encyclopaedia Britannica* of 1797 recommended that frogs be kept in a tub of water to show how swimming should be carried out.

In 1794 a method of upright swimming had been recommended by an Italian, Oronzio de Bernardi, but throughout the early years of the nineteenth century unquestionably the accepted method was the breast-stroke. About 1840 some swimmers began to move their arms alternately, but retained the breast-stroke leg kick. These leg movements were modified over the next few years, leading to the English side-stroke. The date of the 'single over-arm stroke' is about 1855, and what was known as the North of England side-stroke was recorded in 1880. This was described in full:

> The legs are not extended on either side to their full stretch. The upper leg moves about half way on either side giving a vigorous kick on either side (kick not wedge), the orbit of the upper foot forming a figure of eight. While this leg takes the stroke, the under leg pursues an independent course, it does not move out backwards but simply kicks down from the knee joint, the orbit of the foot forming a half-loop of the figure of eight, terminating where the feet meet.

Sort this out as you like. One of the great disadvantages of early teaching books was the absence of helpful illustrations, and, often where engravings are used, the message is vague and frequently tempered by the incompetence of the hack artists who were employed to do the drawings. Typical of such illustrations were those done to illustrate the Serpentine Swim instituted in 1864, in which a large number of swimmers appear to be thrashing away in no recognisable mode. An interesting vignette shows 'the treatment of the apparently drowned', which seems to involve stretching out the arms of the casualty, though what happens then is doubtful except that there is a clear indication that when the casualty, apparently drowned or not, has recovered, he is tipped back into the water to continue the swim.

Those involved in the resuscitation are captioned RHS, evidently the Royal Humane Society, founded in 1774 for the recovery of persons apparently drowned. By the time of the establishment of the RLSS it had 270 depots provided with rescue apparatus, the main one being on the north side of the Serpentine on a plot of land given by King George III.

There were more new strokes and variations appearing throughout the century, especially the trudgen stroke, more commonly known as the trudgeon stroke. This was known in Europe as Spanish swimming, and was made prominent in England in 1873 by a swimmer named J. Trudgen who said that he had come across it while in South America. However, it had been known to a writer named Clias as early as 1825 who had named it 'the Thrust.' Be that as it may, Trudgen's speed was so great that many other swimmers copied him, and it was from the trudgen that the modern crawl stroke grew. The Americans in due

Below:
The Serpentine had its own club

SPLASH!

'It is a notorious fact that almost every swimmer, good, bad, or indifferent, makes a most ludicrous and careless plunge on starting for a race, and at entertainments succeeds in saturating those who are unfortunate enough to be near the edge of the bath.'

The Swimmer Magazine, 1 Mar 1884

course improved the leg kick and breathing techniques and the 'American crawl' became the basic style used throughout the world.

When swimming, Trudgen himself kept on the chest and lifted the upper part of his body out of the water at each stroke. At each swing of the arms he pulled himself forward, resulting in a swirl of water as each movement was completed. The arms were brought forward sideways, each completing a circle on each side of the body, with the head kept completely above water. Those who copied Trudgen found that it was less laborious to use a double overarm stroke with the head and the chest well down, using the ordinary overarm leg kick, and it was as fast. At first it was considered that the trudgen stroke was only useful over short distances and for the sport of water polo where speed was of the essence, but gradually it was discovered that it was a useful all-round method, with men and women swimming fifteen miles using this method and only this method.

A variation arising from the trudgen stroke was the trudgen crawl, in which the arms recovered alternately out of the water and the legs made an up and down beat between each 'trudgen kick.'

The crawl stroke was not generally known in Great Britain until 1902 when it was introduced by Richard Cavill of Australia who came to compete in the English championships. It is said that he acquired the skills after seeing the swimming of South sea Islanders. The crawl stroke was taken up by the American amateur champion, C. M. Daniels, who not only won the English championship but established a new record for the 100yd in 1907 with a time of 55.4sec. The first Englishman to cover 100yd in less than a minute was J. H. Derbyshire.

The crawl stroke is distinct from most other forms of swimming, and a contemporary writer — none other than William Henry, the founder of the RLSS — described it in full and with a precision and clarity not fully realised by other writers of the time on the subject:

> The legs from the knee upwards are kept in line with the body and almost closed; there is no opening of the legs or drawing up of the knees as for the breast-, back- and side-strokes. The swimmer lies flat upon his breast on the surface, the lower part of the legs from the knee downward are alternately lifted above the surface up to the middle of the calf and then they are struck down upon the water with the instep with all force possible. This striking is done from an upward to a downward direction, one leg at a time. The arms are used somewhat similarly as in the trudgen stroke, they are bent at the elbows, dipped in just beyond the head and drawn smartly backwards till they come out of the water at the hips. The right arm is dipped in when the left foot strikes downwards and vice versa.

The result of the movement is that when one or other of the limbs is pulling or propelling the body through the water at the same moment another limb is being recovered for the next stroke, and less resistance is caused in the line of progress. In performing any other stroke most of the limbs are recovered through the water.

This lengthy extract demonstrates that William Henry, to many even in the RLSS a shadowy figure, knew, to say the least, what he was writing, lecturing, and talking about. He was not merely an amiable and wealthy amateur with a philanthropic idea, as many good men and women were who began movements and societies in the 1880s and 1890s, some ill-timed and destined to come to grief, some still with us after more than a century.

As the founder and first secretary of the RLSS whatever William Henry writes is of interest, even if only to establish him as one of the most objective writers on swimming of the time. He maintained that the most useful of swimming techniques is the breast-stroke, and was pleased that this method had been taken up in the teaching of children and young people, preceded by land drill. If one was thrown overboard, particularly if wearing clothes, the breast-stroke was invaluable, and although by the time Henry was writing at the end of the last century speed swimmers looked upon it as obsolete, it was certainly the best for long-distance swimmers, and the acquisition of this skill, together with the backstroke, has saved many lives.

When learning the breast-stroke, wrote Henry, the first thing to avoid is undue haste and rapidity of movements, probably born of nervousness, an important factor to consider when teaching the young. Many boys and girls have been, metaphorically, thrown in at the deep end, their innate fears not fully appreciated by their instructors. This is especially true of public schools where trepidation on the part of the youngster is equated with cowardice.

A 'GRIPPING' TALE

'The event occurred in a bath on the Rhine, and one of the competitors, who was swimming under water, miscalculated the distance, rushed up to the end of the bath, and pushed his head between two bars of the iron grating. The account states that the man was under water two minutes, and being very powerful, he ultimately bent the bars a little and extricated himself.'

The Swimmer Magazine, 1 Mar 1884

Rapid action of the arms does nothing but exhaust the learner swimmer

There is a tendency for learners to thrash about, tiring them and perhaps inciting them to panic

Rapid action of the arms does nothing but exhaust the learner swimmer, the consequence being that the breathing becomes hurried and uneven, leading to lack of the necessary buoyancy. William Henry was most insistent in his teachings that tuition should be carried out with tact and awareness that some people find the movements necessary for swimming awkward and unnatural.

All beginners, he found, tried to make their limbs too rigid, causing stiffness and cramp, and most learners found it difficult to time their breathing. He emphasised that the inhaling should take place during the backward sweep of the arms, and once this important fact is understood and acted upon, most beginners will have little difficulty and their confidence will be greatly increased. Learners also tended to hold their breath for two or three strokes, and nothing was more calculated to exhaust the inexperienced swimmer. William Henry also stressed the need to keep the body as level as possible along the surface of the water.

Opposite:
Although this one has been up-dated, many of the swimming baths of today owe their genesis to the Public Baths and Wash Houses Act of 1846

For those who were able to swim on the breast, Henry considered that it was just as easy to swim on the back, for the leg action is similar and the use of the arms is almost the same. The difficulty

WHY BOTHER?

How many swimmers drown because they don't bother to breathe? This may seem an odd sort of question, but in 1961 a doctor considered the question. Normally underwater swimming is ended when the swimmer has an irresistible urge to breathe. But the doctor, writing in the *British Medical Journal*, related experiences he had had:

'After swimming about 30 metres I realised I had no desire to breathe and felt I could continue for ever. My mind seemed separate from my body, which appeared to swim automatically. I was able to reason that to continue must be dangerous, and so surfaced at 40 metres, taking a few shallow breaths only, in contrast to the usual gulp. For the next four hours I noticed a dull headache.'

with the backstroke was chiefly steering and it was recommended that an object be placed as a guide before swimming, and the head slightly turned in transit so that the object can be kept in sight. The backstroke was partly superseded by the back crawl, and a notable feature of the development of supine swimming was the change in the arm recovery from the straight arm of early days to the 'bent arm recovery' on to the 'relaxed fling' in which the arm is almost straight once more.

At one time, previous to the introduction of the trudgen, the overarm, and the crawl, the sidestroke was the main racing technique. In this method, the body is placed on the side, the upper arm worked from the head to the upper side of the body, the lower arm taken downwards through the water to the underside of the body, and kick made with the legs scissor-fashion.

For a considerable period three styles, back crawl, breaststroke, and crawl stroke, were the accepted racing categories. Speed swimming records were constantly being broken. Great Britain had been pre-eminent in speed swimming, but the Australians and the Americans were beginning to establish themselves. In 1877 the mile amateur record was 29min 25.5sec, and that stood until 1892, the year after the establishment of the RLSS. By 1907 this had gone down to 24min 42.6sec. The 100yd record had also been drastically revised, from 1min 16.75sec in 1878, 1min 6.25sec in 1888, to 55.4sec in 1907.

The first official list of world records was established in 1908, the year of the London Olympics, after the foundation of the FINA (Fédération Internationale de Natation Amateur), and earlier records were examined to see if they could be ratified. Without adequate time-measuring equipment, records tabulated to tenths of seconds were intrinsically suspect.

Some of the events where so-called records were established are astonishingly early. Australia claims to have held the first national championship, a 440yd event, in Sydney in 1846, and also a world championship in Melbourne in 1858, won by Bennet from Sydney who beat Stedman of England. But it was England which is generally considered to have staged the first 'real' national championship in 1869, the victor being a man named Morris who won the one mile freestyle in the Thames. The first United States championship also covered a mile, and was held in 1877.

A very significant event occurred in 1869 where at the German Gymnasium in London the Metropolitan Swimming Clubs Association (MSCA) was formed. In time the name was changed to the Swimming Association of Great Britain, and then to the Amateur Swimming Association (ASA). By 1902 the ASA handbook ran to 300 pages, and the number of swimming clubs had increased from 40 in 1886 to 550 in 1902. To give this figure some reality, nearly 2,000 clubs were registered in 1939. The ASA's predecessor, the MSCA introduced ground rules, defining amateur status, and laying down rules for competitions—vitally important

The competition depicted on this print dates from 1872, soon after the formation of the Metropolitan Swimming Clubs Association in 1869

as, with so many swimming styles and variations of styles, there was a chance of the whole question of competitive swimming becoming chaotic.

That this nearly occurred is clear from the fact that up to the present well over a hundred different events have been recognised for world record purposes at one time or another. Some of these events have long been obsolete, such as the 300yd and 300m freestyle, recognised from 1908-48, 500yd and 500m freestyle (1908-52), and the 400 and 500m breast-stroke (1908-48). The classic distance, of course, was 100yd for all strokes, but in 1956 this was decimalised, and the international 100m (110yd, 100.584m) was substituted, to the annoyance of many of the old school. The imposition of metres instead of yards still rankles with many, not only in the world of swimming but in athletics and other sports as well.

It is clearly evident that swimming was very popular indeed throughout the nineteenth century, though it was not until the National Swimming Society came into being in London in 1837 that the sport received any newspaper coverage. An enormous fillip had been given to the sport in 1828 when the first indoor swimming club in Britain was built in Liverpool near St George's Pier, filled by the rising tide and definitely unchlorinated. But even more important was one of those now-forgotten acts of Victorian altruism, the Public Baths and Wash Houses Act of 1846, which enabled local authorities to build baths using money from the rates and without reference to London.

So far as swimming for the masses is concerned, the main event

DEEP BREATHING

An expert on underwater swimming declared:

'Even if you do hold your breath a long time, it is the first half of the breath that counts.'

Underwater fishermen often seem to be able to hold their breath for an immense time, but, as the expert said, 'The time of actual breath-holding was probably limited to the vertical descent lasting a few seconds. The remainder of the underwater period was spent in a gradual exhalation lasting no more than thirty or forty seconds.'

was 1891. Not, in this context, the formation of the RLSS, but the recognition by the Board of Education that swimming should be a subject of instruction for schools, although there was no attempt at enforcement and it remained merely a recommendation.

Many of the great public baths in the towns and cities, such as the marvellous terracotta public baths cum public library in Moseley Road, Birmingham, date from around this period, when there was a great emphasis on education for the masses in all subjects. However, it was not until the Education Act of 1918 that local authorities were empowered to establish school swimming baths.

The provision of swimming baths for all was vital to ensure that everyone had the chance to learn to swim. However, instruction depended on circumstances. In some baths there was no supervision, no encouragement to learners, and this attitude persisted well into the 1930s and perhaps still does. There is also the fact that insufficient attention was given to the creation of a false sense of security. Many men and women — and especially children — found that swimming in public baths, with controlled depths and clear water, was not so difficult, and in due course tried out their skills at the seaside, in rivers, or, most dangerous of all, canals. Thankfully the RLSS, with their literature and pamphlets, together with the wide publicity for the Blue Code and water safety, has done much to urge even those confident in their abilities to retain their common sense.

AN ELECTRIFYING STORY

In 1988 a city council was fined £1,000 under the Health and Safety at Work Act 1974. Why? Conduits covering electric cables had completely corroded. How? Because of the action of water and chlorine. Where? At the city's swimming baths. 'It did not take much imagination to realise the risk to people using the pool or working on the premises,' said HM Inspector of Factories. Perhaps the understatement of the year.

The widespread proliferation of public swimming baths gave an impetus to competitive swimming at local levels. Competitions were easy to organise, were not upset by weather conditions, and could be equitably judged. However, there was no great audience participation, nor was there until the arrival of television. The main public interest in swimming was connected with distance swimming, and especially cross-Channel swimming, where the contest between man and nature was at its most dramatic. The first man to swim the Channel in either direction, Captain Matthew Webb, became a popular hero, the first swimmer to be known throughout the country — even throughout the world.

The ceremony of Channel swimming also appealed to the public — the greasing with oil (porpoise oil in the case of Captain Webb) the accompanying small boats, and the immense fortitude and stamina needed, as well as patience when the projected speed was no more than one and a half miles per hour. Not the least of the attractions was the chance for newspaper reporters to indulge in painting the scene, as evident in the account of an eye-witness in *The Country Gentleman's Newspaper:*

> The weather was all that could be desired . . . There was not a ripple in the water, and the horizon was obscured by haze, which clouded the swimmer's head from the heat of the sun . . . By 4pm, he had swum five miles and the NE stream

began to tell very strongly . . . The swimmer took some beef-tea, topped up with beer, at 5.38 . . .

Another factor that guaranteed public attention was ever-present danger, not only from exhaustion, but from drifting seaweed, and jelly fish.

Webb was not the first to try. The first recorded attempt had been made by J. B. Johnson in 1872, who started from Dover but only remained in the water for 65 minutes. Webb himself had made an attempt on 12 August 1875 and was in the water for 6 hours 49min before rough weather forced him to call the attempt off after approximately 16½ miles. On 24 August he tried again, diving from the Admiralty Pier, Dover, and ending up on Calais sands 21 hours 44min later, without touching artificial support of any kind, and having covered 39½ miles.

Captain Matthew Webb, the first man to swim the English Channel

As William Henry said, 'it is the greatest swim ever recorded', and although many more attempted it it was many years before the Channel was again crossed. In 1877 Frederick Cavell claimed falsely that he had swum the Channel, and on the strength of this published a book *How to Learn to Swim* with 'press reports of his swim from France to England and Other Long Swims'. In 1879 he emigrated to Australia and helped to develop the Australian crawl. It was 36 years before Webb's achievement was repeated; 71 had tried, including 22 women, but all had failed, including Jabez Wolffe who tried 20 times, three times getting within a mile of the shore, and once he was obliged to retire only a few yards from the coast. Each candidate for immortality had their individual methods; some used the trudgen, others the Australian

Southport sea-water baths, opened in 1871

BEST YEARS OF YOUR LIFE?

Swimming instruction at the schools of today varies enormously. Sometimes there is none. It is interesting to look at the attention given to swimming a hundred years ago at the great public school of Rossall:

Regulations
(1) Every boy (unless specially exempted on medical grounds) must practise swimming on half-holidays in the summer term until he can swim the length of the bath, 40yd, ending at the deeper end where the depth is 7ft.
(2) No boy may bathe in the sea until he has obtained his first-class swimming certificate, which must be signed by the sergeant instructor of swimming, and by the honorary master of the baths.

continued

crawl, Wolffe the overarm side-stroke, and Montague Holbein the backstroke as being the least fatiguing, though it did not help him succeed.

Webb did more than anyone to put swimming, any swimming, on the map. Swimming had become, with Webb, a romantic and fascinating activity. *The New York Times* was just one newspaper to emphasise the effect on swimming by Webb's feat:

> The London baths are crowded; each village pond and running stream contains youthful worshippers at the shrine of Webb, and even along the banks of the river, regardless of the terrors of the Thames police, swarms of naked urchins ply their limbs, each probably determining that he one day will be another Captain Webb.

The life story of Webb was well known — how his first

This was a Channel swim that failed, despite the large audience. It was an attempt by J. B. Johnson in 1872, who bet £30 against £1,000 that he could do it. He managed 7 miles in 1 hour 5 minutes.
Puzzle: find the swimmer

swimming opponent had been a Newfoundland dog whose owner had boasted about the dog's extraordinary staying powers in the water, how Webb had taken the dog on and after an hour and a half in the water was still fresh while the dog had to be taken on board a boat.

Whilst in the Merchant Navy Webb had spent two hours diving and re-diving beneath his ship, stationary in the Suez Canal, seeking to cut loose a rope fouling the ship's propeller. While on the Cunard liner *Russia* he had jumped overboard to try to rescue a seaman who had fallen from the rigging. He failed, but he was presented with a gold medal by the Duke of Edinburgh on behalf of the Royal Humane Society.

His fame was enormous. He was immortalised by Bryant & May on their matchboxes, commemorative china was produced with his portrait on the various pieces, he was accorded a place in Madame Tussaud's and, although he had plans to become an

continued

(3) The tests qualifying for this certificate are as follows:

(i) Each candidate must swim, at the same attempt, eleven laps of the bath, or 440yd. Of these laps, three must be swum on the back; the whole distance must be completed within twelve minutes.

(ii) When starting, the candidate must dive from the platform at the deeper end, which is 6ft high, and swim under water for15yd.

(iii) After completing the required distance, he must, before leaving the water, float without using his arms or legs for three minutes, and 'tread water' for two minutes.

A boy who satisfied the examiners earned the privilege of wearing special 'bathing drawers', blue and white.

Captain Webb's great swim encouraged unqualified swimmers to venture out into open waters, such as rivers and estuaries

inventor, these came to nothing and he made a living in swimming, floating, and diving exhibitions and in endurance tests, despite warnings that he was overdoing it. He anticipated the work of the RLSS by demonstrating survival flotation and lifesaving methods. In 1883 he went to America to swim the rapids and whirlpools beneath Niagara Falls, and drowned. His tragic death added to the myth.

Although the cross-Channel swim was unquestionably the most dramatic long-distance event, there were others which, because of their siting, had greater audiences. One of the most popular was the 'Swim through London', from Richmond lock and weir to Blackfriars, instituted in 1907 and won by J. A. Jarvis of Leicester in a time of 3hr 24min 6.8sec. In this inaugural race 34 started and 21 finished the distance. As one might expect, early long-distance swimming (now defined as distances over 1,500m) was organised on a fairly casual basis, but the rulings of the BLDSA (British Long Distance Swimming Association) brought order. The BLDSA organises many annual competitions in the UK, one of the most demanding being the Lake Windermere race of 10.25 miles (16.5km). Occasionally the BLDSA stage a Marathon-length competition on Loch Lomond (22 miles, 35.4km),.and a 16 mile (25.7km) event on Lake Windermere.

'Most of the principal races are decided in baths', wrote William Henry in 1908, 'but there has been a tendency of late years to revert to open water in the summer and also to encourage long-distance swimming.' He reckoned that open water swimming, and especially swimming in the sea, was the best training and practice for those who really loved the sport — or art, as he expressed it — because they were able to swim under normal climatic conditions and not in the tepid water of a swimming bath, though whether this was a recommendation appreciated by all his readers must be open to doubt.

The tendency towards open water swimming, however, led to danger, and those who had learned to swim in swimming baths had no conception of possible hazards such as weeds and undercurrents. When getting into a bed of weeds William Henry said that the swimmer should stop kicking and work with the arms, relying on the current to get him or her through, as otherwise the weeds will entangle the legs and put the swimmer 'in an awkward plight.' Much of Henry's advice has stood the test of time, and present-day text books often echo his words, almost as though he had written them himself.

As with all sports, swimming techniques were refined continuously to achieve the maximum effect with the minimum exertion, and it might be supposed that by the early 1900s and the London Olympic Games of 1908 most of the permutations had been gone through. Today in competitive swimming there are four recognised styles — the front crawl, the fastest, known in the rule books as freestyle: the backstroke; the breast-stroke; and the butterfly.

STERLING EFFORT

Cheshire is fortunate in that physically handicapped children are catered for in three special swimming pools. A raised rim prevents wheelchairs falling into the water, there are wide margins around all sides of the pool, and there are sloping ramps into the water with additional handrails.

When getting into a bed of weeds, said William Henry, stop kicking and work with the arms, relying on the current to get the swimmer through. Even the humblest stream can present hidden hazards

Although 'Swedish acrobatic springing' had its first recorded championship in 1889, sensational straightforward diving had been popular for many years as is evident from this 1840 poster

SOUTHWARK BRIDGE

NOTICE!!

ROSE & BELL, BANKSIDE.

SAMUEL SCOTT

THE CELEBRTED

American Diver,

Is open to all the World, to Leap or Dive with any Man, for the Sum of

ONE HUNDRED QUINEAS

The Diver will go through his Extraordinary Perofrmanees from off a Scaffold, 160 ft. on the Southwark Bridge, head foremost into the water; you will also hear him Talk as he is descending. The Diver will show many Feats of Agility up aloft, also in the water, on

MONDAY, the 21st Instant,

and during the Week, excepting Christmas Day, & the following week, on Monday & Tuesday at Two o'clock each day. This Celebrated Jumper has Dived from the top gallant yard of her Majesty's hine of Battle Ship, the St. Joseph, in Devonport, Lead first, the height of 200 ft., and was Patronized by the Port Admiral and Officers: off a high Cliff in Cornwall, at Port Reef, 240 ft. high, into 8 ft. of water; at Port Isaac off a Cliff, 304 ft.; at Liverpool, 167 ft.; at Manchester, 100 ft,; at Port Kips, 297 ft.; at Albany, 130 ft.; at Troy, 110 ft.; at Whitehall, in the Lower Port of Canada, 300 ft.; at Philadelphia, 200 ft.; at Baltimore, 167 ft.; at Pattison Falls, 497 ft. and off a Scaffold on Brighton Pier, 140 ft. This well known Man throughout the World, has, through his Perseverance, saved many of his fellow creatures from a watery grave, and has brought up many a man from the bottom who has been drowned.

This Wonderful Prodigy of Nature, may be seen at the Club Room of the above House, where Accommodation will be provided by the Landlord, Mr. SPARKS, for those Ladies & Gentlemen who may wish to bring their Children and Friends to see so Extraordinary a Man, unequalled in the annals of History.

Decr 1840 J. W. PEEL, Printer, 9, New Cut, Lambeth, opposite the Victoria.

THE FIRST LONDON BATHS

The first public swimming baths in London were opened in Green Street, Leicester Square in 1849. This was followed by baths in Lisson Grove, and at Great Smith Street, Westminster. By 1852 there were seven public baths in London. It was estimated that they had been used by 800,000 bathers.

There are also events in which all four styles are combined in one race, known as individual medley, as well as team races (relays) for freestyle only and for medley. In theory, freestyle can mean anything except backstroke, breast-stroke, or butterfly, but in modern racing competitors equate freestyle with the front crawl.

William Henry would have been acquainted with most of today's swimming methods with the exception of the butterfly, discovered in America in the early 1930s by enterprising swimmers who found that there was nothing in competition rules to prevent them recovering their arms over instead of under the water. At first, the swimmers employed the frog-like leg kick of breast-stroke simultaneously with the flying arm action, but this proved tiring and most of the butterfly swimmers were men. Over 200m it was found difficult to maintain the out-of-the-water arm recovery, sometimes impossible. In 1952 the butterfly stroke was deemed a new acceptable style and separated from the breast-stroke, and with this approval the butterfly stroke was refined by substituting a simultaneous up-and-down flutter kick.

Most lifeguards will be acquainted with the various swimming techniques and with the associated sport of diving. This may be necessary, though it is usually advised that the best way for a lifeguard to enter the water is the less spectacular feet-first method, or sliding down the bank or parapet.

Diving in the present sense — which William Henry thought should be called 'springing' and someone more pedantic 'Swedish acrobatic springing' — is of fairly recent origin, and the first recorded major UK championship was that held in Scotland in 1889, which included diving from the side of the bath, diving from about six feet, and a surface dive. High diving became popular amongst a group of dare-devils, and in 1895 the National Graceful Diving Competition was started, open to all comers, and comprising standing and running dives from 15 and 30ft, a competition which continued without break until 1961. In the 1890s fancy diving was introduced from Sweden, where acrobatic and gymnastic diving had been carried out for some years (as it was in Germany as well). This proved so popular that as a direct result the Amateur Diving Association was formed in 1901, largely due to the enthusiasm of Sir Claude Champion de Crespigny, a pioneer diver.

Fancy diving was included for the first time in a competition in 1903, and there was a springboard event in the 1904 Olympic Games for men only. Women participated in Olympic diving for the first time in 1912, though 'plain and fancy' diving from the high board for women was not introduced into the Olympic Games until 1928. Diving lent itself to all kinds of stylistic variations, usually named after the person who devised them. Most of the more eccentric dives were soon forgotten, along with their inventors, but a few stayed the course, such as the Isander (reverse dive) and the Mollberg (reverse somersault).

There was some conflict between the diving and the swimming fraternity, but in 1935 the Amateur Diving Association was wound up, and diving was incorporated into the canon of the Amateur Swimming Association.

So far as lifesaving is concerned, perhaps the most useful form of diving is surface diving, because it enables the swimmer to find and bring an object to the surface. The correct method of carrying this out is to swim a few yards on the surface using the breast-stroke, take a breath, then suddenly depress the head and look downwards. At the same time the body is raised at the hips, and simultaneously a powerful stroke is made with the legs and an upward stroke with the hands. This will give sufficient impetus to send the swimmer down to approximately twenty feet. Once under the surface the swimmer keeps the head depressed and

SCIENTIFIC SWIMMING

William Henry, the founder of the RLSS, won the Scientific Swimming Championship several years in succession. What exactly is scientific swimming? Basically it means unusual ways of propelling oneself, diving, and tricks. These included:

Treading water
Revolving on the surface
Swimming like a dog
Sculling (swimming on the back)
Somersaults
Double somersaults
Marching on the water (not really!)
The propeller
The pendulum
Porpoise swimming
Imitation of the torpedo
Imitation of the spinning-top
The Steam tug
Swimming hands and feet tied
Smoking under water
Eating under water
Staying under water

SWIMMING AT ETON

In many spheres of life, the stable door is bolted after the horse has fled. This applies to the teaching of swimming. There was no organised swimming tuition at Eton until 1839 when a boy named Montagu was drowned by being dragged out of his boat by a barge rope. The man who started the scheme was a celebrated tutor of the time named George Augustus Selwyn, who rowed in the very first Boat Race in 1829 and who later became Bishop of New Zealand and then Bishop of Lichfield.

uses the breast-stroke while he or she searches. When about to ascend to the surface the head is turned backwards, eyes upwards, and a vigorous stroke is made with the arms and legs.

Plunging can also be of use to lifesavers. This is a standing dive made from a firm take-off, face down, body motionless. Never so popular or spectacular as diving, plunging had its championships and its devotees, and one advantage to lifesavers is that it can be carried out anywhere and unlike diving it will not disturb the water surface too much, perhaps important if there is a body or other object to recover. To avoid disaster to those plungers who overestimate their abilities, in 1893 a time limit of a minute was laid down for the plunge, but even with this proviso plungers were able to descend to a depth of 80ft and more.

Swimming can be a sport, can be a method of getting from one place to another through water, and can be a means of avoiding drowning. Many people who drown are not in the water of their own accord. For those who have not learned to swim, there is an alternative survival method. This is, simply, floating.

Many swimmers, oddly enough, find it difficult, even impossible, to float. In learning to float even experienced swimmers, let alone learners, find difficulty in overcoming the tendency of the legs to sink. A beginner can acquire confidence by getting someone to hold the legs up, or failing that to use the steps or the rails of the swimming bath so that the balance of the body can be judged. Before doing so the swimmer should completely fill the lungs, spread legs wide, then lie backwards with the arms extended in a line with the body and beyond the head. The palms of the hands are upwards, with as much weight thrown beyond the head as possible.

The key feature of this procedure is stillness. The back must not be hollowed, the abdomen must not protrude above the surface, something of a task for the generously endowed. The swimmer may sink occasionally for the briefest of periods, but if the breath is held he or she will bob up again, so that the lips are raised above the water enabling ordinary breathing to go ahead. Many people who try to float expect to lie with most of their body above the water, as in old illustrations, but only the face, chest and toes should appear above the surface of the water.

If a learner, having released his grip on the rails or steps, finds that his feet are still sinking, more weight should be thrown beyond the head and turning it well back, at the same time lifting the hands out of the water. This will raise the feet. A knowledge of this invaluable technique would save many lives of non-swimmers, and floating can be practised in a small area of water, even the do-it-yourself polythene-lined children's garden pool, where the ability to touch the bottom at any time will give the apprentice floater confidence. As in many fields (not only swimming), panic, and not the limitations of the human body, is the main enemy of survival.

The Lifeguards' Tale

THE UNITED KINGDOM STORY

The Lifeguard Corps was formed in 1932 and by 1937, the membership was 11,000, many in flourishing and well-equipped clubs. Since 1891 the work of the Lifeguard Corps, later designation the RLSS Lifeguards, has succeeded in reducing the number of drownings by at least 75%. In 1879, in excess of 3,500 people drowned in the United Kingdom, by 1980, this had dropped to around 900. These are the brief statistics, but give no indication of the dedication and the sheer hard work put in by thousands and thousands of men and women in their spare time. The majority of open water lifeguards are unpaid and their only recompense is the knowledge that they have saved life, often the lives of the young who are most at risk in the water.

Lifeguarding is one of the three main areas of work undertaken by the Royal Life Saving Society UK, the others being water safety education and individual rescue skills. There are three categories of membership of RLSS Lifeguards, namely Lifeguard, Cadet and Associate and all members are required to be members of a registered lifeguard club.

What then makes a good lifeguard? Lifeguards must be fit, have confidence in their own abilities and those of their colleagues and be able to work both on their own and as part of a trained team. They must also have a sense of humour and a strong vein of patience, for they are dealing with the general public, individual members of which will be at pains to demonstrate their independence and will resent any attempt to tell them where or where not to swim; if they decide to wade out into six-foot breakers on an ebb tide there will be no way to dissuade them if their minds are made up.

Training in open water is essential, for no matter how good a swimmer or how strong a lifeguard may be, the uncertainties and unreliability of the sea, river, or lake cannot be foreseen in the safety of the swimming pool. Caution is another essential quality,

A BUOYANCY VEST

A valuable aid to safety was exhibited at the 1989 London International Boat Show. This was the new Hotline buoyancy vest in geometric designs with dazzling colours, and featuring deep-cut armholes for freedom of movement, and multiple straps to make certain that the vest stays in place.

The use of a line by a team of stalwart men who know what they are doing is a long tradition in lifesaving. This is a 1901 interpretation

for a lifeguard can easily put his or her own life in peril when trying to rescue someone who is plainly bent on self-destruction. As with basic lifesaving rescue skills, the self-preservation of the rescuer is of paramount importance. However, with specialist training, rescue equipment and support from others in the team, the lifeguard is able to deal with far more serious situations than the individual lifesaver.

There are two basic situations a lifeguard may encounter — the mass accident and the individual accident. The first type is rare, for collisions of ships, ferry-boats and pleasure vessels usually take place during a storm or in fog and only rarely will they come within the scope of the RLSS Lifeguards or within a patrolled area, although occasionally, mobile units may be called to assist with such occurrences. If an individual member of a club is involved — perhaps as a passenger, perhaps because he or she happens to be on the spot — there is every likelihood that the training the lifeguard has received will allow him to remain calm and do what can be done to assist. Doing what can be done may mean throwing out lifebelts, it may be assessing what can be used in lieu of lifebelts (such as empty plastic containers) and using those. Being able to assess a situation is vitally important.

Sometimes there are mass incidents rather than mass accidents. In 1981 the South Humberside Life Guard Club was on duty at the Festival of Long Distance Swimming and had to deal with no fewer than 21 casualties.

Opposite:
Lifeguards must be fit and have confidence in their own abilities

Lifeguards of one kind or another have been in existence for many years prior to the formation of the RLSS. The naval gentleman on the left of this 1872 print is clearly keeping an eye on what is happening in the swimming pool

UNFAIR COMPETITION

In the late sixties and early seventies the Ramsgate Lifeguard Corps, during patrol duties at weekends at the Western Undercliff used to have a practice/demonstration run of reel and line drill, and I can well remember one Sunday being 'casualty' for the team. I swam out some thirty or forty yards, took up my position and gave the signal to shore. As the sea was lumpy I continued with the swim so that the beltman would see me. I saw the beltman approaching, and then out of the corner of my eye I saw another swimmer approaching from my right. As he approached, what did he say?

'Keep calm — I'm a lifesaver.'

I explained the situation quickly, and he swam off muttering something about playing b . . . lifeguards!

Colin S . Hudson

Individual accidents are much more frequent. There are a hundred and one possibilities, constantly added to as aquatic leisure activities continue to grow. Common accidents in the sea include being hit by a surf-board or wind surfer, small boats and canoes capsizing, people falling from wharves, piers, rafts and the banks of rivers into the water.

In addition, of course, there is the task of rescuing people in difficulties whilst they are bathing, swimming, or even paddling. To the public at large, this is the quintessential duty of the lifeguard, though it must be emphasised time and time again that far more people are drowned away from the sea than in it.

Why do accidents occur? This is almost on the level of the question 'How long is a piece of string?' There is an almost unlimited set of replies. Drink, stupidity, showing off, recklessness, over-confidence, immaturity or perhaps faults in equipment, whether it is a boat or something else. Accidents can happen to the most sensible and alert person, for the unpredictable is always just around the corner. This applies not only to someone in difficulties but also to the rescuer or potential rescuer. It must always be remembered that a person under the influence of alcohol is more likely to fall into water than someone who is sober. A drunk person is even less likely to react in a reasonable fashion to a rescue attempt than a panic-stricken, sober individual.

When a lifeguard club takes on the responsibility for looking after a stretch of water, no matter where it may be, the members must know and understand, to the full, their individual and collective capabilities. This is, in many ways, a lot to ask of anybody. That there are thousands of people willing to do this may seem, in an age where everyone stands a chance of being accused of utter selfishness, to be extraordinary.

Another important attribute is observation, and the ability to make sense of what he or she sees. If someone falls off a pier or jetty, there are several factors to consider. If it is a pleasure pier at the seaside and the lifeguard has not had the opportunity to study the structure at low tide, there could be underwater hazards. It is likely that the struts and foundation members are of cast-iron and may be in a rusty or damaged condition. If it is a working jetty, there are likely to be mooring ropes hidden from view and also seabed debris. If the jetty is in a fishing port the hazards can include broken crab- and lobster-pots, which can operate as mantraps on a victim's or rescuer's leg. There may be the screws and propellers of small craft and even an outboard motor can be a danger if the vessel is swaying at anchor.

Sometimes common sense will help. A swimmer in difficulties in the distance or mid-distance will most likely be a fair swimmer, for otherwise he would not have got that far in the first place. A non-swimmer in difficulties in the distance is more of a priority and a rescuer has to weigh up the chances of getting to him in time.

One of the duties of the lifeguard is to be aware of potential hazards. These breakwaters may seem quite benign. But if they are covered by the tide, if the bases have become littered with debris?

In all cases, even if it takes a little longer to launch and row, a lifeguard is advised to use a boat rather than swim unless the casualty is in great distress and within a reasonable distance from the shore. If the rescuer swims a good distance he or she may subsequently be unable to surface dive to retrieve a casualty.

The equipment a lifeguard club has available varies from place to place. Some clubs operate on a very limited budget, some have the financial backing of a benevolent local council. Some clubs achieve incredible feats in raising the necessary money. The Gosport and Fareham Inshore Rescue Service Club saved for three years, raising £25,000 to purchase an inshore lifeboat powered by two 80hp Mercury outboard motors with a top speed of over 35 knots. They are 'on call' 24 hours a day in liaison with the local coastguard.

The club was fortunate in that it received sponsorship and the boat was named *Grace Sparshatt* after the late wife of the sponsor — that is the clue to the making of a reasonably wealthy club — the ability to promote it so that businessmen and other people will contribute towards its finances.

The kind of boat depends on the funds available. It can be a rowing boat, a powered boat, or, for certain waters, a canoe. The RLSS UK strongly recommends that canoeists engaged in rescue work need to be trained and qualified by the British Canoe Union, as canoeing is not a simple equivalent to rowing in a lightweight

Why do accidents occur? This was a staged incident with no risk which went wrong. Not every occasion has a press photographer at hand!

boat. A rowing boat needs a certain amount of expertise, but not much. The main thing is to get into it facing the right (or as it happens, wrong) way. It does not have propellers so there is less likelihood of inflicting injury to victim or to the rescuer who has jumped in. And the rescuer can bring the casualty in over the stern, thus reducing the risk of the boat capsizing.

When a lifeguard club has acquired a boat it is necessary to equip it and those who are in it. Life jackets should always be worn and so should warm clothing, preferably lightweight so that it is easily discarded in an emergency. A first-aid kit suitably waterproofed is a must, as are throwing and towing lines. A boat-hook is not only useful for manipulating the boat but also for hauling casualties aboard; a horn may help if there is fog or mist and it can act as a signalling device. A loud-hailer can be employed both to help casualties and to communicate with other rescuers.

There are a variety of flares. A smoke flare can serve as a marker, a hand flare can be waved to attract attention and a parachute flare gives general illumination. Seas may be rough and, as most boats ship water at some time or other, a bilge pump or some form of bailer is necessary, as is a fire extinguisher in a powered boat. In addition there are the common sense items, the tools in case the engine fails, heavy-duty knives in case wires or ropes need to be cut, waterproof torches and unless it is a lightweight inshore vessel, a compass. The provision of a sea anchor obviously depends on the type of boat.

Of course, all types of vessels are used in rescue, often depending on what is available at the time. Inflatable boats can be

The type of boat a club has depends largely on the funds available

SECOND TIME AROUND

In 1988 a former hotel waiter in Torquay rescued a three-year-old boy who had fallen into the icy waters of Torquay harbour. 'When I started to revive him he was completely blue and I couldn't open his jaw. I saw another man pumping him but I knew he was doing it too hard — with young bodies you have to be careful not to damage their lungs.' The rescuer had learned lifesaving in Portugal, and it was the second time he had rescued a small boy from drowning.

Portrait of a lifeguard as depicted in a short publication from the time when the RLSS was located at 8 Bayley Street, Bedford Square, London

'HELP! I CAN'T SWIM!'

A colleague and I set up an incident for a police lifesaving competition at the Canterbury Pool, which involved a plane crash. The crew had bailed out, and one of them had his parachute entangled in some overhead obstruction (the high diving board). He was still in his parachute harness dangling about a foot above the water, face down and unconscious. The other two crew members got into a dinghy — it was very realistic as they were in full flying gear. The two in the dinghy were in fact members of the Search and Rescue helicopter crews from RAF Manston, but the man in the parachute harness was a trainee fireman from the MOD Fire School at Manston. All went well until towards the end of one of the incidents the time whistle was blown before the parachutist had been successfully placed in a position of safety, so the rescuer who was in the process of 'towing' him simply let go of the casualty and swam to the side of the pool, whereupon, much to our horror, we heard a plaintive call from the water 'Help! I can't swim!'

How's that for guts? And, of course, we then had a real rescue on our hands!

Colin S. Hudson

invaluable because they have low rounded sides and no sharp edges and it is therefore easier to get a casualty aboard. Fast craft may be all very well, but for general patrol work they are heavy on fuel. Attention must also be paid to ease of transport and a fibreglass boat may be more convenient than a wooden one if it has to be carried on a roof-rack. Surfing equipment can also be used in rescue. The surf-board can act as a boat, as a float to which the victim can hold, or as a resuscitation platform.

The jet-engine boat is recommended as the best choice, although expensive. It is fast and has the advantage that it has no propellers and is therefore safer for someone in the water. Where a lifeguard club has a rescue boat it is important that there is liaison between the RNLI and the Coastguard service or the police for inland waters. It is pointless to duplicate duties and if there is no clear understanding between the various rescue bodies there is a danger of complacency — the belief that someone else may be doing the job when in fact they are not.

Much of the money needed is raised by jumble sales, sponsored swims, raffles, dances, discos or perhaps by having a float in a carnival. In addition to a rescue boat, what other equipment is a club likely to need for its lifeguards?

Authorities affirm that the torpedo buoy is essential, and is considered by some as the number one rescue aid. It can be used as a towing aid for a tired swimmer and the flexible version can be wrapped around someone who is totally helpless.

There may be the need for a means of marking out patrol areas in the water, using perhaps a set of buoys although frequently the home-made variety is as effective and cheaper. Some form of communication equipment will be needed, which may be by two-way radio such as CB, or perhaps simply a loud hailer or mega-

The importance of maintaining close links between the rescue services, the police, the ambulance service, the coastguards, can never be stressed enough

An impressive turn-out of lifeguards. The flag of the North Worcestershire lifeguards on the right shows that strong branches can be built up well inland

phone. Most clubs would accept the need for some form of transport and would like custom-built Range Rovers; the majority however have to be content with what they can get — maybe even an old Austin A30 with a roof-rack!

Advice on all matters concerning RLSS Lifeguards is available from the specialist volunteer officers nominated by the National Lifeguard Convention and details may be obtained from the society's headquarters.

What then is the role of the RLSS Lifeguard?

The principal role of the lifeguard must be to encourage and promote safe activity on, in or near water. This is achieved in many ways which may include: advising on hazards and dangerous conditions, to observe and where necessary, supervise, swimmers, pseudo-swimmers and non-swimmers, to carry out rescue and resuscitation, to look after comrades in the club especially the trainees and to be willing to co-operate and liaise with the other rescue organisations, whether they are familiar bodies or relatively unknown.

Opposite:
Lifeguards, wherever they may be, should know exactly what they are doing, where they are doing it, and why

Lifeguards should know exactly what they are doing, where they are doing it and why. They should be equipped with all the

relevant information — telephone numbers, duty rosters, what auditory or visual warning systems are available and, where applicable, times of high tides and the weather prospects. They should know the terrain and be able to read nautical charts and Ordnance Survey maps, especially the larger scale 1:25 000 versions and know how to find a grid reference quickly and accurately.

There may be blind spots, there may be look-out points; these can often be found by a sensible inspection of a map and there may be places where the public congregates for no apparent reason. Other rescue services may well help in providing such information. Prevention of accidents is often a question of pure common sense; but this may not be enough.

A foot patrol provides evidence that the lifeguards are about and active and ensures that anyone who spots someone in difficulties knows where to go. Where resources are available, watch may be kept from the water, perhaps from a moored boat. In some waters activities are kept separate but often they are not and these are the most dangerous as those people with the most powerful appliances for doing damage are sometimes the most oblivious to those in danger. A buffeting from a wave may not seem much to a jet-skier at speed; but it could be the head of a swimmer instead.

As with all services that look after the public in some way or other, whether it be the police or St John Ambulance, there will be times when nothing at all happens and there is always a chance of boredom or complacency. As voluntary organisations have no formal disciplinary structure, the problems of boredom and complacency need to be countered by relocating the men and women on duty or by giving them alternate jobs.

A lifeguard has to be endowed with common sense on patrol and on watch; even more when something happens. A person who has been trained to rescue a casualty may well have the utmost confidence in his or her abilities but he or she may have too much confidence. The end result may be two drownings instead of one. Two rescuers are better than one and a team is better than two. So team training is a vital part of the lifeguard's curriculum.

In the early days this was done in a severely military fashion, so much so that the drill was often seen as more important than the task for which the drill was designed. A middle way has to be found that produces flexibility with self-imposed discipline. At march-ins at competitions members find that a good deal of pleasure can be obtained from what might seem to be akin to military square-bashing.

More than anything else, headquarters and patrol centres vary from club to club and area to area. A control and communication centre may be a custom-built mini-space-centre with flashing lights and winking computer screens or it may simply be a room with a table, a chair, a telephone and a logbook. The logbook is vital. It provides not only an account of what is going on, but what

WAITING FOR MR RIGHT

On one occasion I was on duty when I saw a teenage girl standing on some steps at the end of a concrete groyne reaching out to another girl swimming and obviously having a little difficulty getting to the steps. I nipped down there smartly, and as I approached I called out to her 'Are you all right?' to which the one on the steps said, 'Yes, we're waiting for a lifeguard.'

'Sorry, love,' I said, 'you will have to make do with me!'

(I was about forty-five years old at the time — the rest of my group were eighteen-year-olds.)

Colin S. Hudson

Water always attracts

has gone in the past; and history teaches, or should.

The lessons of history are many and varied. Techniques and attitudes change and these include the methods of rescue and resuscitation, though from an early age it was realised that rescue can be a traumatic experience for the rescuer as well as for the rescued. The first duty of the lifeguard when called to the scene is to ascertain how serious the situation is; a man marooned on land cut off by the tide is in no immediate danger; a man clinging to an upturned boat is in more of a danger but it is not critical; a child in either situation may be in deadly peril. Someone floating apparently unconscious may have been dead for a long time. Whatever the situation, it calls for speed and decisiveness.

If the casualty is conscious, a non-contact rescue is preferable, as a panic-stricken person can have the strength of ten people and take a rescuer down. One of the main features of rescue training is getting out of the grip of a person who is drowning. If the rescuer has a torpedo buoy or something similar it is pushed out ahead so that the drowning person gets hold of that. If this in some way calms the victim, it may be possible to tow the victim to shore. Breaking waves may panic even a good swimmer because broken water does not give the buoyancy of a swimming pool. So circumstances can turn someone who is perfectly capable of saving him- or herself into a victim.

The rescuer must also be aware that strong waves are his enemy too, reducing his ability to cope, and tiring him.The recommended way of getting through waves is to dive towards the seabed just before each wave arrives, to hold on to the seabed with both hands, feet brought to the hands as the wave passes over. The feet are then used to spring the swimmer up to the surface on the

TAKING A BREATHER

Shortly after the end of World War II Kent County ASA revived its Long Distance River Swim in the Medway from Teston to East Farleigh, a distance of about five miles. Among the swimmers was Charles L. Harrison, a lifelong lifesaver who had gained his Bronze Medallion in 1932, and as he had completed three-quarters of the course he reckoned that he would be well placed among the honours at the end.

Quite close to him he noticed a fellow swimmer in difficulties and immediately went to the rescue, taking hold of the casualty and towing him to the nearest safety boat, holding the boat gunwale with one hand as he assisted the unfortunate swimmer into the boat. He then continued his swim and completed the course, only to find that he had been disqualified for 'resting' whilst holding on to the boat!

A lifeguard has to know how to effect a release from the clutches of a drowning man, as demonstrated here in drill form

far side of the wave. This continues until the swimmer can no longer feel the seabed.

There are several established ways of bringing the casualty to shore, all confirmed by hours of practice. It is often arduous, needing the back-up of a reel-and-line team, supplemented perhaps by willing and able members of the public. This again emphasises the need for team training.

Lifeguards are not often confronted with a mass accident. If they are, they have to make quick and sure decisions. Who is in most danger? Who can manage for themselves? If the rescue boat is in amongst them will they clamber in and throw everyone in the water? Are there children? Are there additional hazards? It may be a ship going down suddenly taking those in the water with it. There may be risk of injury from wreckage. There may be unexplained and dangerous cargo. Is a dive underwater looking for casualties justified? Lifeguards are advised that this is debatable unless the water is clear down to a considerable depth.

There are several methods of underwater search. In shallow waters, lifeguards go in abreast, arms linked, feeling with their feet and using a sweeping action. As with deeper waters where swimming is necessary it is important not to go over the same territory twice, whether the search is in a circular pattern or in parallel lines. In some search cases, rescuers can be towed out by boat and by using a tow-bar up to three swimmers can be used.

Naturally lifesavers on board patrol boats have to be as alert as shorebound lifeguards and are advised not to be side-tracked into collecting beach-balls that have drifted out to sea or be engaged in other irrelevant tasks.

There must be knowledge of customs — what the various types of buoy indicate, the rules of the road at sea and what lights on other vessels mean, and what the accepted sound signals are. There is no question that a fully qualified lifeguard has to assimilate a good deal of information. Hand signals have over the years been systematised so that there is no ambiguity. Hand signalling is especially important if rescues are being carried out using reel-and-line. It must be remembered that when a rescuer is swimming out to a victim his perspective is very limited. It is difficult to judge distances and the sense of direction might have been thrown awry by water conditions.

Lifeguard clubs do not exist in isolation and competitions and championships not only enable members of different clubs to get to know each other but also act as a spur and an encouragement. Thanks to a good deal of hard work many competitions and championships are sponsored. They are an interesting spectator sport and offer a sponsor excellent advertising possibilities, not only in the competition programmes but with on-site displays. A competition can be killed by feeble and amateurish organisation and referees, judges and timekeepers should be one hundred per cent competent and not someone's relation who happens to have

A SLIGHT PROBLEM OF SEX

Among the most unusual applications for lifesaving teaching came from a group of Buddhist monks and nuns in Sussex. As it is not acceptable for these devotees to touch members of the opposite sex, there were, to say the least of it, problems.

a few hours to spare for a worthy cause.

It need hardly be said that organising a competition is a major task. Making certain that officials are available, that there is no clash with other similar events, that the venue is suitable and that the audience will consist of more than an old man and a dog. Changing-accommodation has to be supplied, areas have to be marked out, buoys have to be laid, there may be flags and bunting, first-aid facilities have to be laid on and all the equipment has to be available — starting pistols, stop watches and all the other minor items that may easily get overlooked.

It is interesting to look at a typical event. A good example was the National Lifeguard Championships of 1981 held at Wanlip Park Countryside Club in Leicestershire, sponsored by Ashford Creameries Ltd. There were 72 teams from 26 clubs, some small, some large, some from near the sea and some from inland. The City of Rochester Swimming and Lifeguard Club though it consisted of only 14 lifeguards and 19 cadets entered five teams. Crawley Town Lifesaving Club operated in swimming pools and

A lifesaving demonstration by the Worthing Life Guard Club

lakes. Hounslow School of Lifesaving was one of the strongest clubs with a membership of 300 and a rescue boat on the Thames with which the stretch between Hammersmith and Runnymede was patrolled. The membership of a club does not necessarily mean that all, or even most, are lifeguards; Lincoln and District Lifeguard Club had 150 members, of whom 20 were active lifeguards. Some clubs had specific areas to patrol, others liaised with other rescue services.

Some clubs operated throughout the year, but others only on weekends and public holidays. The Colwick Park Lifeguard Club was formed to provide cover for one of the then new water-based leisure centres in Nottinghamshire and, although formed only two years earlier with equipment consisting of a rope and a pole, the club was so successful in promoting itself and in fund raising that it had provided itself with two rescue boats, an example of what can be done when the enthusiasm and gusto is there.

The competition was in several parts. The key event in the programme calling for more than the ability to swim fast was the 'unknown incident', contested by each team separately. There was one event for men, one for women, one for boys and one for girls. Because the same situation was set for each team in succession the test was carried out at two locations. The unknown incident test involved simulating an accident in water; the team had to employ a wide range of rescue skills, assessing the situation, planning the course to take, dealing with the incident and its aftermath. All had to be accomplished within three minutes. Naturally the teams taking part were kept well away until their turn came and they had no contact with other teams. Judging was based on skills demonstrated, with a time limit so that other events were not interfered with.

The march-in, for men, women, boys and girls separately, was also a feature of the programme, judged on smartness, bearing and turn-out, indicating the degree of discipline of the individual teams. There was naturally the swimming, with teams of four participating, men and women over 800m, boys and girls over 400m. Medals were awarded for both the winners and the runners-up and for most of the events there was a trophy and a cup as well, donated by a diverse range of businesses, individuals, and industries.

Such events place the RLSS UK Lifeguards in centre stage. The annual championship is their showpiece. However, much of their work goes on quietly and without ostentation. There is, in the modern world, no shortage of small dramas; there is too much in the way of major disaster for minor misadventures, even domestic tragedy, to make the headlines. The RLSS Lifeguards occupy the front line of the RLSS UK and any support or sponsorship they manage to attract is small recompense for the tremendous work they do, often in difficult circumstances, often with no outsiders to give them a pat on the back and say 'Well done!'

FALSE ECONOMY

A woman who was rescued from rough seas in the summer of 1988 by two young surfers later asked the coastguards why there was no lifeline rope on the headland. They said 'that it was not worth it because it would mean replacing a series of ropes.'

Opposite:
Competition is an incentive to accomplishment, and a smart turn-out by examiners and participants alike is a great fillip to morale

15m
RLSS
LIFEGUARD

The Future of the RLSS

The future of the RLSS can be summed up by 'the three Ps':

Public Awareness
Professionalism
People

The days have long gone when the RLSS has been vaguely associated with lifeboats, and thanks to thousands of hours of arduous work on the part of volunteers teaching and examining the message has got through, to individuals, to children, and, often through the children, to the parents.

The 3 Ps are closely interlinked, for public awareness is often aroused by the professional approach, by the realisation that what might be called flag-day promotion is a thing of the past and that modern technology needs to be brought to bear to present the RLSS as a long-established yet up-to-date caring body, with a strong corporate image. And the programmes of the RLSS need to be projected, programmes helped so much by a wide variety of sponsors, from banks and manufacturers to insurance companies and holiday promoters.

Many volunteer services of the past have staggered along, kept going by the well-meaning enthusiasm of amateurs. Often there has been a lack of vision, with the administrators tackling each task as it arises and unable, and sometimes unwilling, to stand back and take a cool look at the problems. This has not happened with the RLSS, for at the core there has always been a body of men and women who have done just that, surveyed the situation and decided what needed to be done. So in 1960 it was seen that it was imperative for the branches of the Commonwealth to be brought to the fore, achieving equal billing with the RLSS in the UK.

The professional has the knowledge and experience to know what will work, and the ability to anticipate what will happen in the future. He and she knows that everything will be affected by the move into Europe by the UK in 1992, and this includes the

BREAKING THE PAIN BARRIER

Bryan Simpson, 53, of Royston in Cambridgeshire, was out sailing alone in a gravel pit. It was mid-winter 1988. He saw a youth in difficulties in the water, and dived in, rescuing him, despite the freezing water and the panic of the young man. Nothing remarkable in this? Five months earlier Mr Simpson, a member of the RLSS and a teacher of lifesaving skills for 15 years, had had a heart bypass operation, and carried out the rescue despite searing chest pains that would have sent nine out of ten people scurrying back to the bank.

work of the RLSS. There will be a need to associate more closely with the lifesaving societies of Europe, and a commission is being set up to establish standard qualifications that will be accepted everywhere, something akin to those associated with the Bronze Medallion. The dangers of drowning know no boundaries, and the shores of Lake Lucerne in Switzerland, the sands of the Devon coast, and the shark-infested waters of the Antipodes will be safer if there are lifesavers about, of no matter what nationalities, who share a common purpose and the same lifesaving techniques.

Along with this commendable process is the need to internationalise signs, in which the three great lifesaving societies, the RLSS, the FIS, and the WLS, can all play a vital role. The red flag flying on the beach may obviously symbolise danger, but it is possible that somewhere it does not. And with a standardisation of signs there can be no possible room for ambiguity. It can be done. When Britain's roads were first equipped with international signs many thought that it would lead to confusion, incomprehension, and an increase in road traffic accidents, but in a month or two the new symbols were assimilated and accepted. And so it is with all sensible projects.

Unquestionably there will also need to be a standardisation of equipment, and in research and development there is a vast field

A splendid example of sponsorship;. The South Worcestershire Life Guard Club pictured with the mayors of Evesham and Pershore and other local officials on the presentation of a caravan to the club

'WATER BOARD, MATE!'

While walking along the side of a canal notorious for the fact that over the years several people had fallen in and drowned, a lifesaver saw a middle-aged man huddled in a heap on the ground, apparently in distress. He was watched by a group of children who did not seem to be doing anything. The lifesaver raced up. Surprised, the man looked up from his crouched position.
'Water Board, mate,' he said, 'can you give me a hand in getting this cover up?'

THE NATIONAL WATER SAFETY CAMPAIGN

The National Water Safety Campaign, begun in 1960, was a laudable attempt to encourage lifesaving, swimming and general water safety. At the time there were 792 publicly owned baths of which 328 were open air, and there were 100 more in the pipeline. Schemes were sponsored by Coca Cola and Bovril, and the committee included representatives of :

Ministry of Transport
Ministry of Education
Dock and Harbour Authorities Association
River Boards Association
Inland Waterways Association
Association of Pleasure Craft Operators
Ship and Boat Builders National Federation
National Home Safety Committee
Central Council of Physical Recreation
Scottish Yachting, Water Sport, and Water Safety Advisory Committee
British Association of Organisers and Lecturers in Physical Recreation
River Thames Society
Amateur Swimming Association
English Schools' Swimming Association
Swimming Teachers Association
Institute of Baths Management
Royal Life Saving Society
Surf Life Saving Association of Great Britain
Order of St John

continued

waiting to be cultivated. Great steps have been taken to ensure that there is ready co-operation in the RLSS between the branches in this area. A simple example is the spine-board, invented in Canada to help alleviate the pain and distress of those who have suffered spinal injuries, and that hopefully will be available to all the branches that want it. A communications task force will see to it that there are no barriers to the ready exchange of information on any relevant subject, and problems such as copyright are waived. If someone somewhere produces a better product, injured pride should not prevent it being taken up wholeheartedly.

The aim of professionals is to get it right — and to see that others get it right. A growing area is consultancy, and that presupposes that the RLSS will be recognised as the body with the knowledge to give expert and informed advice. It can be on any subject. A simple example lies in the construction of swimming pools, and the importance of bringing in an advisory committee at an early stage. At one newly designed swimming pool there was a system of arches around the water's edge. It was observed by a consultancy committee that the uprights of the arches, as they were, would prevent the lifeguard standing in the arch from having a complete view of the pool; if the arches were set back a further foot this would not arise — the lifeguard would have all-round vision.

In the sphere of education much can be done, and experts from the RLSS can advise educational bodies how much time should be spent on physical education and swimming. It is worth mentioning that every child in Germany learns to swim, and this should surely be the aim of educationalists not only in the UK but throughout the world — if possible. Loughborough College in Britain is a shining example of how lifesaving can be introduced into the curriculum. In the Commonwealth, RLSS NZ field officers teach lifesaving in schools, and in several countries a lifesaving pack has been included in the schools' national curricula.

It must be remembered that conditions vary so much, and for small countries, including those in the Commonwealth that are without public swimming baths, a well-intentioned programme may be non-operable.

The importance of lifesaving classes in schools can never be overemphasised

Physical disability should not stop a person participating in water-based activities

In the past, when standards were set and handbooks were issued by the UK, some of the instruction and recommendations were not applicable, and certain environmental factors were ignored, and some factors, important in Commonwealth waters, were not applicable in the UK. Not surprisingly many Commonwealth countries produced their own handbooks for use in their own specific conditions. The answer is mental flexibility, to be aware that the conditions that apply to one's own branch or even one's own country are not universal. In the larger countries of the Commonwealth, one state or region can be totally dissimilar to another, and it was very sensible and logical to allow the divisional branches to attain a high degree of autonomy.

As had been observed at Commonwealth Conferences, often very succinctly, without volunteers the RLSS would cease to exist. There is nothing more important than attracting volunteers, not only lifesavers, but educationalists and administrators, and one of the best ways is to convince a newcomer that he or she is not merely being slotted in because he or she happens to be there, but

continued

British Red Cross Society
Royal Humane Society
Royal National Lifeboat Institute
Royal Yachting Association
National Schools Sailing Association
Amateur Rowing Association
British Canoe Union
British Sub-Aqua Club
British Water-Ski Federation
National Safety Education Committee
British Standards Institution
British Waterways Board

It was organised by the Royal Society for the Prevention of Accidents (RoSPA), the Water Safety Organiser of which, Mrs Vera Bryant, said:

'This is a campaign which must succeed for, unless efforts are made to spread a knowledge of water safety and to promote training in the skills of watermanship, we shall continue to suffer these pointless deaths by drowning.'

Did it succeed?

More than a quarter of a century later the RLSS published a leaflet called *Ten Ways to Drown a Child* opposing cuts in public and school swimming and lifesaving provision. In 1960 one in seven schools had no provision for teaching children to swim. This was thought horrendous. What are the figures today?

Co-operation between lifesaving services all over the world is demonstrated in this photograph where a group of lifesavers from Fermanagh went on a visit to Bielefeld, Germany, to liaise with German lifesavers

that a career pattern can be formed, and that the RLSS can be a path for personal development. At the RLSS UK summer schools this is increasingly being emphasised, with the accent not only on lifesaving but on other activities not normally associated with the society.

Volunteers want responsibility, self-respect, and recognition, and this has long been appreciated, though often shown only on occasions where members have received honours. Honours have always played a major part in the RLSS, and all branches use the same society or Commonwealth honours, such as the Certificate of Thanks, though some branches supplement these with their individual awards.

The Service Cross (which can be supplemented by a bar) and the Recognition Badge (with bar) have long been eagerly sought after, and a permanent way to denote appreciation has been to appoint honorary life members, honorary life governors, and vice-presidents, in ascending order.

A sense of responsibility is of course requisite for members of the society wherever they may be. A person's life may depend upon it. But responsibility itself, the taking on of burdens without being asked or instructed, may be more difficult, for it may involve an unusual degree of self-examination. Developing one's own resources, and, even more, discovering one's own resources, can be a fascinating journey.

A fascinating development in the RLSS is the concerted effort to encourage the more active middle-aged and elderly people to join the society, many of whom have their own specialist skills — perhaps in education, perhaps in communication — to contribute. Often such members, who may have been searching for a role after they no longer need to go out and earn a living, have had to make major decisions in the course of their life. And, whether for the young or old, decision-making is vitally important. Some decisions may be easy; some may be hard; and some may go counter to one's natural instincts, as for example in helping people to help themselves rather than taking the easy option and doing everything for them.

This is particularly relevant to members of the RLSS involved in assisting small or newly formed Commonwealth branches, where a good deal of persuasion and subtlety may need to be used. In Africa, there is often an ingrained belief that voluntary work is somehow wrong, and that such duties, especially those relating to lifeguarding, should be paid for.

Fortunately the governments of many of the emerging states are realising the advantage of lifeguards and the necessity, in the interests of tourism, to keep their beaches safe, and these governments are eager to make use of the expertise offered to them

SUPERSTITION

The RLSS aimed to promote common sense about swimming, drowning, and rescue, and attempted by education to counter superstition.

In the very year the RLSS had its genesis as the Swimmers' Life Saving Society what was described by William Henry as a painful case of superstition in action occurred in County Donegal. About ten in the morning two young ladies went to bathe. The tide was on the ebb, and there was an undertow. The ladies were seen to be in distress, but before anyone could go to their rescue they had drifted out. A brother of one of them dashed out, but he himself had to be rescued. A boat was put out from the pier but it was too small for the heavy waves and a larger one was launched. The boatmen reached the two women, one of whom was supporting the other. One of the men took hold of a leg. And then dropped it. For it was possible that one or other of the young ladies was dead, and it was unlucky to take a corpse on board a boat — forever after there would be no successful fishing. So they towed the two women to land 'as if they had been logs of wood.' When the boat reached shore the men refused to do anything; it was unlucky if they got wet bringing a corpse to land, and so bystanders, horror-struck, had to do the job. Needless to say both the women were dead.

Young members of the Leicester branch of the RLSS UK proudly showing off their newly acquired awards. Recognition guarantees an on-going interest

Among future priorities is consolidating the position of the RLSS as the leading authority in water-safety education, and to continue to be the trend setter in safe aquatic recreation

without let or hindrance by technical advisers of the RLSS. These experts may have to conquer prejudice, and be sufficiently flexible to communicate information in a simple down-to-earth manner. As long ago as the first Commonwealth Conference of 1961, the Nigerian emissary conveyed the frustration of enthusiastic lifesavers trying to get to grips with the terminology of the standard handbooks.

Forward planning is not easy, for there are sure to be imponderables that arise fortuitously. The Commonwealth branches have produced laudable long term plans in which the demands of the future have been expertly predicted. Among the priorities is consolidating the position of the RLSS as the leading authority in water-safety education, and to continue to be the trend setter in safe aquatic recreation. Another necessity involves increasing the membership and developing a membership package, including

Litter is one of the curses of life today, whether it is in the street, countryside, or on the banks of a river or canal, where it can prove more than a nuisance and eye-sore but a positive danger.

benefits and a membership card.

For many years it has been stressed that the way to obtain new members is to go out and get them and not wait for them to drift in (and possibly drift out again). New members are the life blood of a voluntary organisation.

Naturally other organisations are anxious to attract recruits. The RLSS has to offer the more challenging deal. And there is no question that it will succeed in doing so.

On the future of the RLSS, the Commonwealth Chief Secretary, John Taylor, would refer questioners to the simple prayer:

'O Lord grant me the serenity to accept the things I cannot change; the courage to change the things I can; and the wisdom to know the difference.'

Wise words for the 1990s and beyond.

POPULAR SPORTS

The most popular sport in 1973 was angling; second was swimming with 2.75 million participants.

The branch president of the Staffordshire branch of the RLSS UK giving instruction to a group of children at a Newcastle school. These are the RLSS members of the future and the place of lifesaving in education cannot be over-emphasised

Drowning – Facts and Figures

What is drowning? It might be said that everyone knows. But is it true?

Drowning is the result of asphyxia, due to the stoppage of a supply of fresh air to the lungs. There is an amount of stationary air in the lungs, and into this is diffused oxygen from the fresh air taken in, while the carbonic acid, which it has taken from the blood through the walls of the capillaries, is driven out. This process is carried out continuously, and is regulated by the brain. When a person who cannot swim goes under water there is a natural tendency to struggle; in the effort to breathe, water is drawn into the lungs, the drowning person coughs, expelling not only the water but the air. In further efforts to breathe more water is drawn in and has to be swallowed.

The oxygen in the lungs is diminishing, the quantity of carbonic acid is increasing, and at length the air in the lungs is too impure to effect an exchange with the blood. The blood passing into the heart becomes venous (deprived of oxygen), and this is sent out to all parts of the body instead of arterial blood. The respiratory nerve centre is affected; the victim feels a dull sickening pain at the back of the neck and insensibility occurs. The face of the person becomes dark and congested through the veins being gorged with blood. The heart stops.

In a paper called 'The Mechanics of Drowning' in the *Royal Naval Medical Bulletin* of April 1960 the writer admitted that the mechanics of drowning were far from being fully understood, and that reports on drowning and near-drowning cases were required with X-ray examinations and full blood investigations. The paper investigated the cases examined where there was a glottic spasm, and the lungs remained dry, likely to occur 'where the reflexes are brisk.' There were also differences between those who drowned in salt water and those who drowned in fresh water.

Primitive mankind did not know anything of this, and did not,

RESURRECTIONISTS

In 1959 eleven lifesavers in Durban were 'killed' medically and then brought back to life in tests to save lives on South African beaches. Volunteers were anaesthetised and paralysed to stop breathing and then subjected to the respiration tests. Results were 'extremely satisfactory'. This was also done in America. There were fifty volunteers who were anaesthetised, and injected with curare, as used by South American Indians, which paralyses the breathing muscles, and, indeed, all the muscles in the body. The air to the lungs was then provided by a rubber tube inserted in the windpipe.

When a person goes under water there is a natural tendency to struggle, and take anyone down who happens to be near. A patient and accomplished lifesaver can relieve the panic

or could not, engage in learned debate. But they could see what was happening, even if a degree of interpretation took place. Certain myths were propagated; that a drowning person would rise three times. Each individual case of drowning depended on the circumstances; the victim could be entangled in weeds and underwater hazards; the victim could die of shock on being submerged.

Only in modern times were the right questions asked.

From 1961 until 1973 the Royal Life Saving Society UK published analyses of fatal drowning accidents every two years from information supplied by Chief Constables. These covered England, Wales, Scotland, and Northern Ireland, though in 1973

WHICH WAY UP?

'Is that boat supposed to be like that?' asked the woman. It was a polite tentative enquiry, as if she thought she might be making a fool of herself, and the ferryman casually looked. No, it was not supposed to be like that. It was an upside-down canoe being swept rapidly down river, and there were two bobbing heads in the water. The ferryman managed to haul the two eleven-year-old boys on board his ferry. There may be a future in boat recognition courses for the public, with learned instruction on which way up they are.

Northern Ireland was excluded.

From 1975 to 1980 the Scientific Advisory Branch of the Home Office compiled and published drowning statistics based on police reports from the forces in England and Wales. This information supplemented details about drowning available from mortality statistics. In December 1980 the Home Office decided that it would no longer collect all this data, and so the Royal Life Saving Society UK with the co-operation of the police decided to carry on the work, and publish their findings — a sterling task that is still carried on.

It is interesting to review the information gathered from the period 1975-80, bearing in mind that unquestionably there was under-reporting. So although there were approximately 700 drownings a year reported, the true figure, for both inland and coastal waters, was perhaps nearer 900. To give this figure,

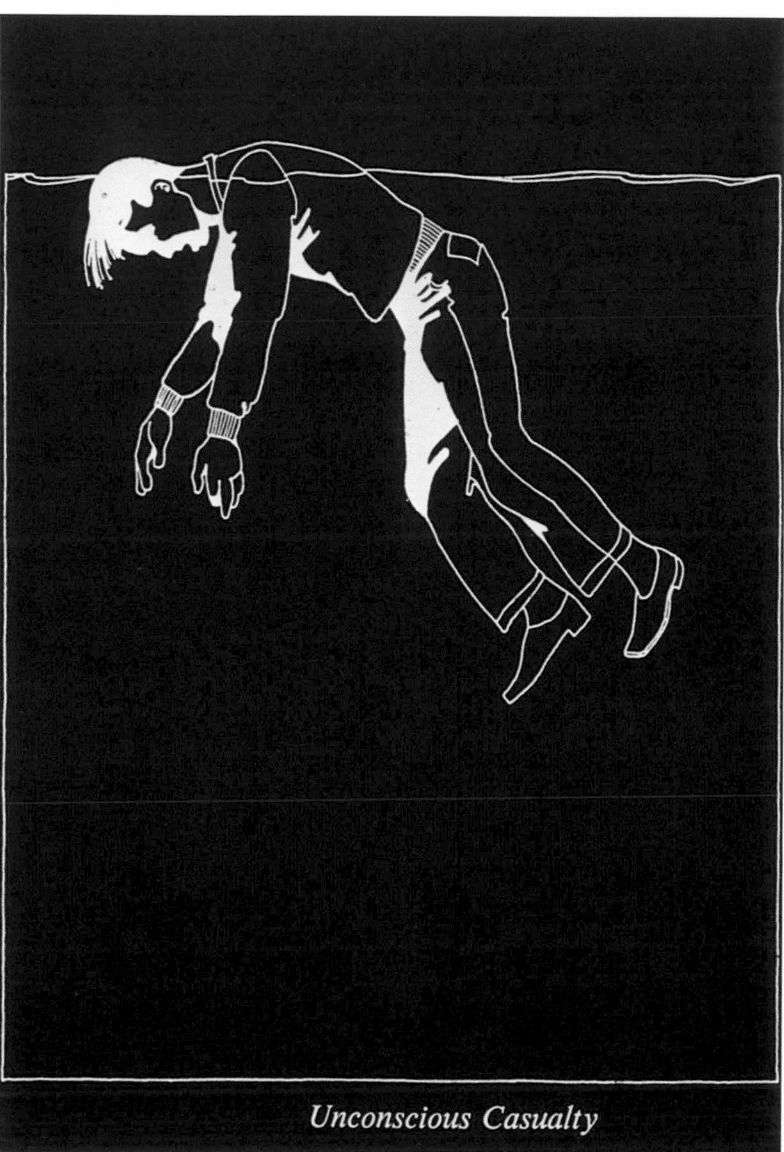

This is how an unconscious or dead casualty floats. In heavy seas he or she is often difficult to see

although sombre enough, some perspective, in 1879 3,690 persons were drowned in England alone, in 'internal waters', and by accident, though how this can be determined is impossible to say. This represented .55 per cent of all deaths. As a comparison, matters were much worse in the Merchant Navy, when between 1876 and 1879 an average of 2,225 men drowned every year, 1.13 per cent of the sailors in the mercantile marine.

There are some surprises in the 1975-80 statistics, especially to outsiders who believe that most drownings take place in the sea. More men than women drowned, at a ratio of three to one. This is exactly the same ratio as 1879. As might be expected, the most vulnerable are the very young and the elderly, with young men between 20 and 39 not far behind. Ten per cent of drownings occurred in the bath, mainly women, but most drownings occurred in rivers and the sea. One in three occurred in rivers, one in five in the sea, one in ten in lakes and other large bodies of water, one in twenty in swimming pools, and one in twenty in coastal waters including estuaries and docks. Ponds, ditches, brooks, streams, pools, and of course canals, also took their toll.

Many people who drown have no intention of being in the water at all, and these include people at swimming pools. In all such statistics there is bound to be an area of ignorance. However,

It is a surprising fact that most people who go out in boats can swim. Yet this does not stop them getting drowned. As William Henry said a hundred years ago, open water is vastly different from the friendly swimming pool

NOT MUCH TIME

'In an ordinary case of apparent drowning the rescuer may have only about twenty seconds before the coming of irreversible cardiac failure.'

The Practitioner, July 1960

'ULLO, 'ULLO, 'ULLO!

Not every successful rescue attempt ends in gratitude. In August 1895 Mr Henry Charles of Arcadia Street, Poplar, London jumped into the Thames to rescue a woman, 'whom he has no means of identifying beyond the fact that she weighs about fourteen stone. He formed an estimate whilst she was doing her best to drag him down with her. However, he did land her safely at last, and then she told him to go away as she wanted no more of him.' In the rescue attempt Mr Charles had lost his hat and boots. So he jumped in the Thames to try to recover them. He was 'rescued' with 'great difficulty' by PC 75E, and appeared at Bow Street Magistrates Court charged with attempted suicide. (The case was dismissed.)

it was known what the swimming abilities of half the number of victims were. Most people in the water could swim, most people in boats could swim (a surprise), and most people who had fallen in the water or who had been land-based in some way were non-swimmers (no surprise).

Of course, there are contributory factors. An elderly person taking a bath alone is always at risk, and senility and the inability to appreciate or cope with danger accounted for a large number of the drownings. Physical disability accounted for one death in twenty among men; rather less among women. Among young adults up to the age of 24 alcohol had been a contributory factor in about a quarter of the drownings, although when the RLSS UK began to compile their reports it was found that alcohol was a significant factor in 47 per cent of drownings in the 20-30 age group. Among young adults stress and mental depression accounted for a sixth of drownings; these percentages were reversed with older age groups.

Although women had a good safety record, half of those drowned were afflicted by stress or depression, but only one-fifteenth of the women had had recourse to alcohol.

The logical question to ask the Home Office in 1980 was what ministers and those in authority were going to do about it. And the logical answer may well have been 'What can we do about it?' Naturally it is impossible to regulate against crass stupidity or carelessness. A person who is drunk may or may not take a meandering course home along a river bank or canal side, and if a person is mentally disturbed or deeply depressed he or she is in little danger of being targeted as someone likely to drown. A person who is going to commit suicide in water is not likely to advertise the fact unless it is a mock-attempt to gain attention or sympathy.

What did emerge unquestionably was the absence of notices warning of danger, but here again it is difficult to place blame on any person or groups of persons, for it would be impossible to

Heroic Rescue

Kenya rescue 1987

A poignant message is conveyed in the form of a letter from a young Kenyan girl:

There were some boys who went swimming with their cousin who did not know how to swim. As they were swimming he watched what they did and tried to do the same. As he tried to swim he did not succeed and all the children who were swimming shouted for help.

I heard the words 'Drowning, drowning' so I took a rope which was near to me (because I saw people were just running with empty hands) and when I reached the edge I saw all the people looking at the boy as if they were afraid to swim and help. I threw the rope to the boy and told him to catch it. It was hard for the boy to remove his hands from the water to catch the rope but, through God's help, he succeeded and some men helped me to pull the rope until the boy was on the river bank.

I tell you, you could not believe your eyes when the boy was out of the river. The parents gave me fifty shillings which I used to buy exercise books.

Fooling around in boats can be dangerous. Fortunately not here with the RLSS boat nearby

raise notices except at recognised danger points — and such danger points may not be apparent except when a tragedy occurs. An analogy may be made with roads; an accident black spot is not a black spot until something occurs.

One of the most dangerous water hazards of all is the canal. A hundred years ago there were 3,124 miles of them (as opposed to 1,786 miles of river). Canals are deep and there is usually no clear demarcation between the canal and the bank except perhaps a kerb of bricks or stone; and although canal lengthage is now drastically reduced, the prospect of erecting systematic warning signs along them must be virtually nil. It is equally impossible for canals to be systematically patrolled.

In the end, the only remedy is for people to take more care. And if they do find themselves unexpectedly in water, or in surprising difficulties in water, to be able to survive. Defensive driving is now a well-established term; 'defensive living' may be worth adding to the treasury of useful phrases.

The reports sent by the police forces of the country to the headquarters of the RLSS UK can make gruelling reading. And the meticulous reports issued by the RLSS UK continue to surprise the reader. In 1982 66 per cent of children under the age of sixteen who were drowned were not supervised by an adult. An incredible 73.5 per cent of those up to and including the age of four were

It is impossible to put up warning signs everywhere. But here is a good one – clear and succinct

not accompanied by an adult. Most of these young children were drowned playing near water and, as might be expected, none of these was able to swim.

If this highlights one ominous factor it is that adults simply do not recognise that water can be dangerous. There may be reasons for this. The natural environment is increasingly under control, and people are insulated against that fact that nature can be hostile. There is also a blithe belief in the 'it can't happen to my family' syndrome, and when it does it comes as an even more shattering blow.

A remarkable finding is that in 1982 most people between the

The smile on the girl's face belies what could be a frightening situation

ages of 10 and 39 who drowned could swim. In the 15-24 age group 90 per cent could swim. The question that demands to be asked here is: why, then, did they drown? One reason may be suggested by the previous paragraph. The forces of Nature have been ignored, and the fact that swimming in a swimming pool and swimming in open water are not the same has not been known or, if known, not appreciated. A study of the Royal Navy's 30,000 drowning casualties during World War II suggests that many of them died from cold water immersion rather than from submersion. All water kills; cold water kills faster.

Another reason is that young swimmers are not psychologically prepared for occasions where they may find themselves in difficulty and, as with non-swimmers, have forgotten what they know and have panicked. Even the most hidebound non-swimmer should be aware that if disposed in the right manner in the

YOU DON'T SAY?
'Some of our best swimmers are inveterate smokers, but such a practice, as any person will readily admit, is not one calculated to improve the staying powers in any marked degree.'

William Henry, 1893

This is one of a set of water safety posters produced by young school children in the Seychelles. Wherever there is water, there is danger

CURING SINUS TROUBLE

How to cure sinus trouble:
Swim to the bottom of the pool, holding the nose closed firmly with the fingers and, with the mouth closed tightly, inhaling as hard as possible. This creates a negative pressure at the entrance to the sinus which, when combined with the positive gas pressure inside and the external water pressure outside, sometimes causes the sinus to drain immediately.
Thanks, I'll stay with my sinus.

water he or she will float rather than sink. This was emphasised in the 'drown-proofing' technique largely initiated in America, 'a revolutionary concept of water safety (where) anyone — young or old and even the non-swimmer — can be virtually insured against drowning.'

Drowning statistics by their very nature are bound to be incomplete, and all findings have to be regarded with a certain amount of circumspection. However, some facts are clear. More than twice the number of people who drowned in rivers in 1982 were walking ('en route on foot') rather than swimming. More people drowned in boats on the sea than those who were swimming or paddling (27 as opposed to 24), another somewhat surprising statistic. Most people who drowned in canals had been walking along the bank; only one person was actually drowned whilst swimming in a canal. But throughout all reports, and not merely the one year 1982, the percentage of people who could swim and yet drowned continues to astonish.

This should surely mean that swimming instruction should somehow be rerouted, and that more emphasis should be centred on swimming under difficulties. And, of course, there is the psychology of the swimmer, a question that has perhaps received too little attention. The ASA (Amateur Swimming Association) has given the matter some consideration, as when it studied a typical group of young swimmers who attended the ASA Advanced Swimming Training Course at Loughborough over a course of years in the 1950s.

It found that most of the 13-17 year olds (the age limits for the course) came from solid backgrounds with good educational qualifications (60 per cent from what were then grammar schools, 20 per cent from technical schools and colleges, and 20 per cent from 'modern' schools, which can be equated with comprehensive

Heroic Rescue

Crocodiles — The Reality of Lifesaving
Zambezi River, Zimbabwe —
15.00 hours 1 May 1986

A party of eight people on a canoeing expedition were drifting downstream with some of the group swimming in a reputedly safe area. Jeremy Lloyd, a 13 year old schoolboy, was suddenly taken under water by a crocodile which then surfaced with Jeremy in its jaws. Rupert Nevis, a Coldstream Guards Officer, threw himself towards the crocodile but it again took Jeremy under. Joined by student Alexander Shaw, Rupert groped around in the water searching for the crocodile but Shaw himself was then hauled under, severely bitten and suffered a broken arm. Jeremy's father had now joined the search and, upon finding the crocodile, plunged his own arm into the beast's jaws which enabled Rupert to drag Jeremy from its mouth, pull him to the surface and place him in the nearest canoe. Mr Lloyd had meanwhile been taken under water but surfaced when his arm was snapped off at the elbow. All the injured were removed by canoe to safety and flown to Harare for surgery. For his involvement in the rescue, Rupert Nevis was awarded The Royal Humane Society's Silver Medal; Alexander Shaw and Hugh Lloyd received Bronze Medals.

schools), that they were taller than average, were not faddy, and smoked very little. No one, apparently, drank to excess (though if they did they would hardly confide the fact to those earnest men and women who were conducting the survey). A study of swimmers and athletes in general was conducted in 1961, and it was found that swimmers tended to be more extrovert than average and 'there was no evidence of the neurotic, the schizophrene, or the over-aggressive.'

It may be that extroversion results in a degree of self-confidence, and no doubt a number of drownings are caused by the effort to impress anyone who happens to be around at the time. And an extrovert is less likely to indulge in bouts of self-doubt; this confidence may be very admirable in competitions, but in ordinary life self-doubt can act as a life preservative.

In a surprisingly high number of cases (91 per cent) the activities preceding drowning were known. It might be supposed that men, women and children (and mostly children) playing on rafts and inflatables were particularly at risk, but this does not seem to be so, and was far less dangerous than paddling.

In 1982 there was little evidence that drug abuse played much of a part in the drowning statistics, though this must be an important factor today, and of course there is a much wider range of water activities. Surfing was in its infancy, and where it was indulged in it was an organised sport practised by the experienced. How different today, and how different are the materials with which surf-boards and surf-skis are made. No one needs to be reminded of cheap lightweight affairs that almost have the quality of balloons. Surfing not only is dangerous to the inexperienced who try it, but also to bathers, and lifesavers report that one of the constantly recurring injuries brought to their notice at their beach stations occurs to people, especially children in the water being struck by surf-boards. As jet-skiing becomes even more popular, injuries to innocent bystanders (or perhaps more accurately byswimmers) are bound to increase.

There are some water-based sports which, unlikely as it may seem, are in decline. A hundred years ago skating was a popular sport, and any stretch of frozen water, or in many cases near-frozen water, was immediately taken over by hordes of skaters, anxious to show off their skills. Today, deaths by skating appear to be minimal, and are usually set into that annoying category 'miscellaneous', 'others' or 'various', which seems to indicate that the statisticians are bored or knocking off for lunch. In 1879 147 people were drowned whilst skating (Mulhall's *Dictionary of Statistics* [1880]).

In 1984 The Royal Society for the Prevention of Accidents (RoSPA) organised a National Water Safety Conference, and surprising new statistics were found. Despite the cuts in swimming lessons by local authorities, it was found that there was an astonishing reduction in the drowning figures for the under-

DROWNING STATISTICS MALAWI 1986

Of the 317 drownings recorded,
115 were children and
202 were adults.
They occurred as follows:
16 in Lake Malawi
108 in Rivers
23 in Dams
32 in Wells
138 Others

8 Were attributed to hippopotamus attack
18 Were attributed to crocodile attack
20 Were attributed to canoes capsizing

fifteens. At one time this group contributed a third of the total; in the 1970s it was a quarter; in the 1980s it was down to 12-15 per cent. It led many to the belief that there may not be a certain connection between swimming and safety.

Many of the conclusions of RoSPA had also been reached by the RLSS UK. One of the characteristics of tragedy is the manner in which a chain of events can occur, each link apparently harmless. A typical instance of what is called the drowning chain occurred in January 1982 when a holiday maker from Scotland threw a ball for his dog to chase on the Promenade at Blackpool. Eventually the ball bounced into the sea, and the dog followed the ball. The man tried to rescue the dog by going in after it, and police officers attempted to rescue him. Three people died.

How could all this have been avoided? Perhaps if the man had been better informed, if he had known that during the previous year a boy had been washed away by a freak wave; perhaps if he had kept the ball in his pocket and walked on the opposite pavement. There was speculation that the public should be denied access to such routes when the weather conditions are bad, but this is expecting too much of a local council, especially as waves breaking over the promenade of a seaside town invariably attract a crowd, which also invariably includes a few dare-devils determined to stand up to Nature.

It may be asked why there was no supervision. In the middle of winter? In weather conditions where it would be crazy to try to swim? Lifeguards even where there is a strong club cannot be on

STICK TO KNITTING

For many years mouth-to-mouth resuscitation was regarded with distaste. 'If you are not prepared to do this to save life you should have stuck to knitting or armchair-criticism and not gone in for first aid', declared the medical journal *The Practitioner* in 1960. 'Bacteriologically the well-washed lips of the apparently drowned are much cleaner than the hands of people who are constantly wanting to shake yours.'

Many people who drown have no intention of being in the water at all, and bridges with low parapets and riverside walks can be dangerous, especially to the young and the very old

The President of the RLSS, Prince Michael of Kent being presented with a sponsorship cheque by Tore Laerdal of Laerdal Medical, the leading manufacturer of lifesaving aids and a staunch supporter of the work the RLSS has done, is doing, and will do

duty all the time, even in summer. At some resorts they patrol on weekends and public holidays, and any further activities are impossible. All volunteer services have to recognise that their members have to go out and earn a living and that the time they can devote to the particular service, whatever it might be, is not endless.

There is no question that ignorance and disregard of danger are the main causes of drowning accidents. Sometimes victims cannot conceive of any danger, especially if they are young. If adults, they may consider themselves waterproof. They may be lulled into a false sense of security, not only by their lack of knowledge of the real world, but by an idealised scenario. Very few people drown on television; they are rescued in the nick of time with hardly a hair out of place. In news programmes those who drown are never seen. They don't last long enough to be photographed.

An incredible case of what can happen is furnished by an incident which happened at Overton Lake near Peterborough in 1979. A family hired a large rowing boat and when out in the middle of the lake where the water is eighteen feet deep the occupants decided to change seats. The father stood up, lost his balance, and fell overboard, sinking as soon as he had entered the water and drowning. No one was wearing lifejackets which were

WHAT THE DICKENS?

A case of attempted resuscitation occurs in Charles Dickens's novel, *Our Mutual Friend,* in which:

'Captain Joey, the bottle-nosed regular customer in the glazed hat favours the doctor with a sagacious old-scholastic suggestion, that the body should be hung up by the heels, "sim'lar to mutton in a butcher's shop"!'

A GREAT AIM

Lifesaving! Whose pulse does not quicken, or bosom swell at its mention? What deeds of heroism float across our mind's vision! Will it be our lot to participate in or effect some gallant rescue, and should the opportunity present itself are we fitted to carry any attempt to a successful issue? Those are sentiments which should receive the serious consideration of all who boast a knowledge of the noblest art on earth. Every natant should ask himself this question: Can I, with my acknowledged abilities as a swimmer, turn them to good account in the service of my less fortunate fellow-creature? It goes without saying that the answer should be in the affirmative. But is it so? I am very much afraid that the natants of today, in the main, pay far too much attention to what is known as pot-hunting to give a single thought to that practical use they should so that in case of necessity they would be able to turn their knowledge with credit to themselves and advantage of mankind.

The Swimming Magazine,
1 March 1899

afterwards made mandatory; another instance of closing the stable door after the horse had bolted. It is always a busy time for people who close stable doors.

Another accident occurred in the same lake soon afterwards, and involved a river cruiser, the *Nene Star*, a privately owned riverboat that took up to sixty visitors onto the River Nene and back. One July a group of about forty teenagers swam from the bank or from inflatables and hitched rides or climbed on the roof of the cruiser as it progressed between the lake and the river. This section was narrow with steep sides, and the helmsman could not stop, for otherwise the youths would probably have been crushed. Park wardens were called to deal with the situation but were ignored, and although the police were called they were unable to respond right away.

Fortunately the behaviour seemed to stop, but after a time it started again and once more the police were summoned. As the cruiser re-entered the lake a sixteen-year-old boy jumped from the cabin roof, and tried to swim to shore. He managed to get fifteen feet from one of the park's large 'no swimming' signs and then went under, his cries for help not heard above the noise the other revellers were making. Consequently he drowned within reach of the bank.

The person responsible for the safety of the lake said afterwards that the worry of another drowning was always with him, declaring that the real worry should rest with parents. 'We've had very close shaves with very young children who are literally left to their own resources at the water's edge while mum, dad, etc, snooze, play ball, read the Sunday papers, completely oblivious of the very real dangers they're placing the children in.' When taken to task the parents apologise and take note, but on one occasion a park warden saw two youngsters aged about six and eight swimming next to the 'no swimming' sign where the boy had drowned. They were watched by their father, and when the warden drew attention to the notice he was 'subjected to the most disgusting verbal abuse he'd heard in many a year'.

As the drowning accidents on this lake were so fully documented — not always the case with leisure-centre fatalities — an examination was carried out on the safety measures available, which were 'impressive'. They included a large number of 'no swimming' signs, a park radio service installed at a cost of £4,000, a rescue boat manned by qualified personnel with first aid equipment, while during the peak season the lake was manned by RLSS UK lifeguards equipped with uniforms, lifelines, torpedo buoys, megaphones, and binoculars.

The organisers of this leisure-centre are to be commended for their sterling efforts in the cause of water safety. But how many of the leisure-centres, opening at an incredible rate as supermarkets did in the 1960s, are as well equipped?

It gives cause for concern. And not the least of the dangers today

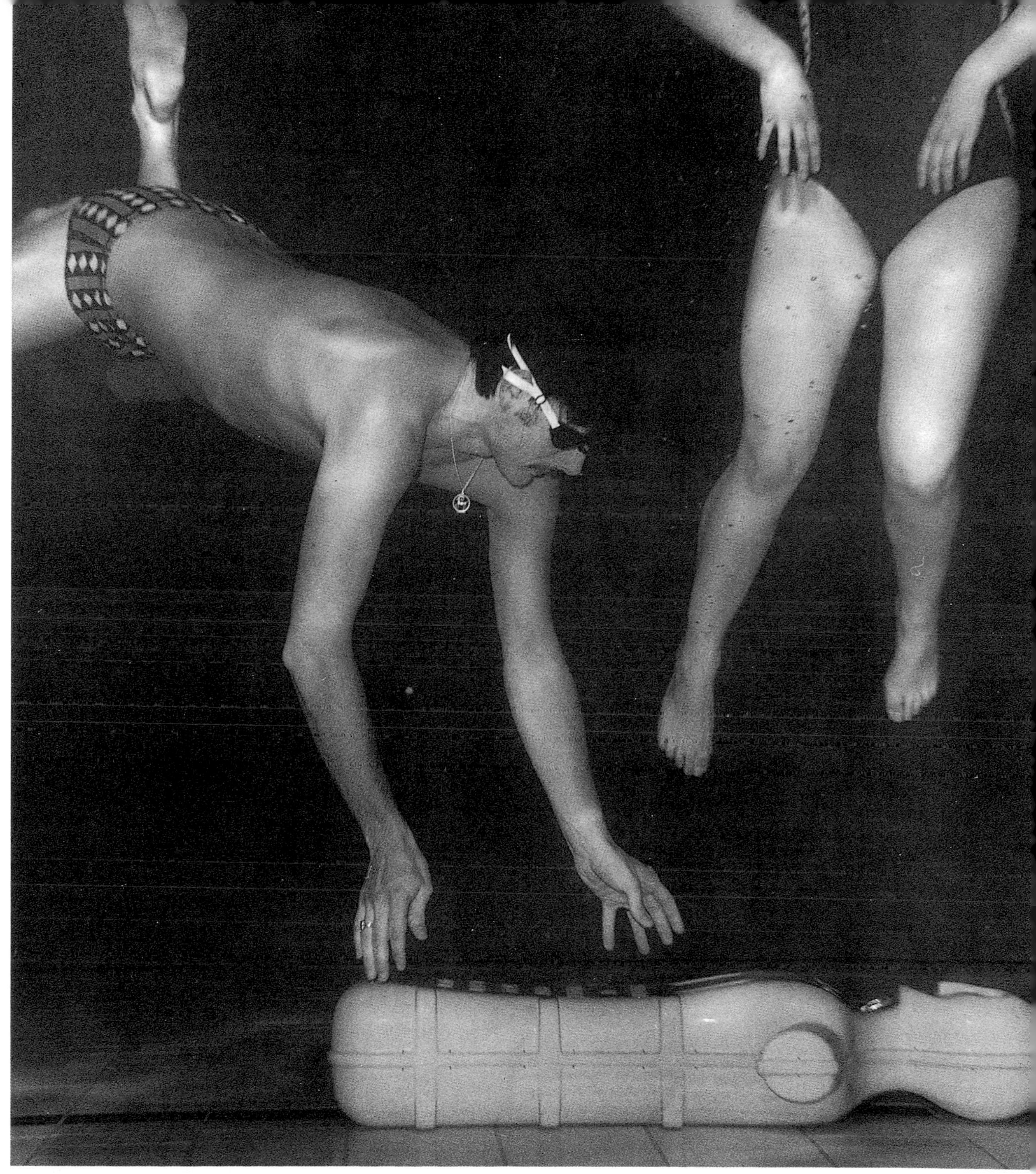

is polluted water. It may be the case that the River Thames is cleaner than it was a hundred years ago, but it is the exception that proves the rule. There is not only pollution from discharges and industrial refuse, but during the hot summer of 1989 there appeared a strange green algae on reservoirs in the South West capable of killing animals. Perhaps the algae was something else to be ignored by the foolhardy.

Underwater swimming is a sterling test of fitness and stamina, but no one needs to be told that recovering a manikin from the bottom of a swimming pool is different from rescuing someone maybe entangled with weeds in a river, or being washed about on an ocean bed

"You throw me the money and I'll throw you a flag."

A cartoon from 1949 with more than a hint of reality in it!

Appendices

A rescuer backed-up by a reel-and-line team

APPENDIX 1

SOCIETY STRUCTURE

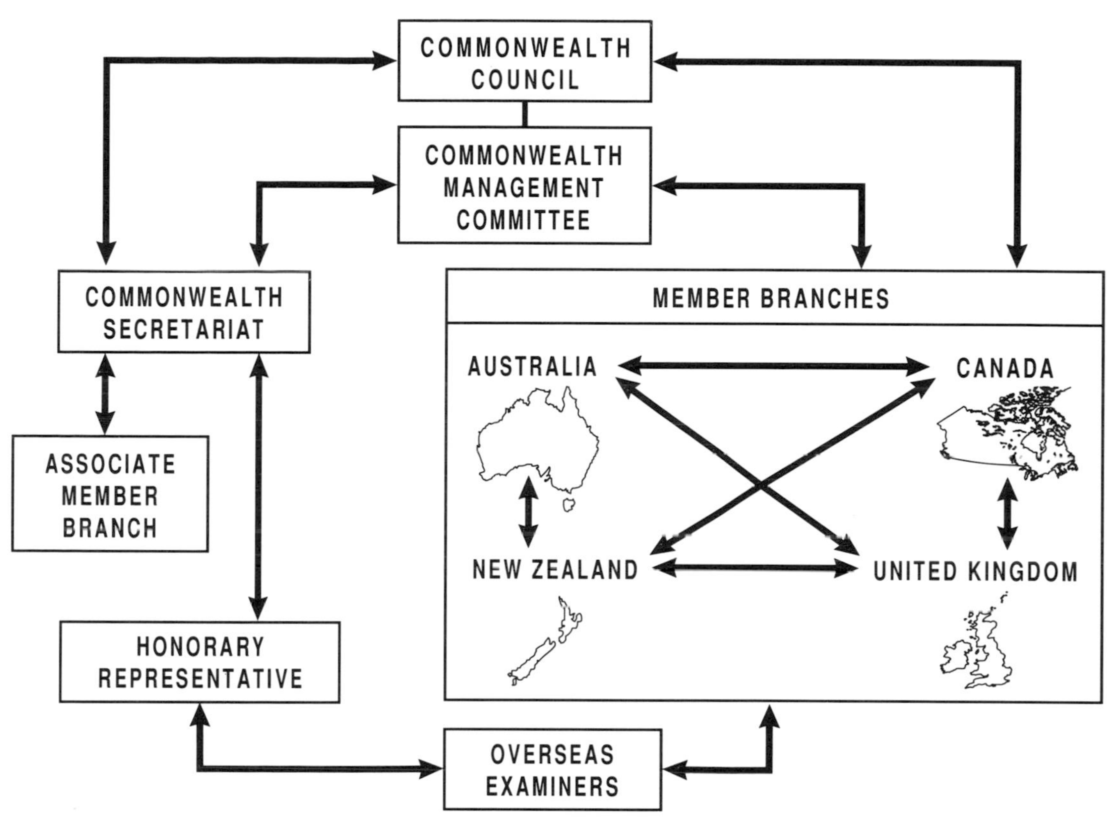

LOCATIONS OF SOCIETY ACTIVITY – 1990

MEMBER BRANCHES [4]

Australia
Canada
New Zealand
United Kingdom

ASSOCIATE MEMBER BRANCHES [11]

Bahamas
Bermuda
Gibraltar
Hong Kong
Jamaica
Malaysia
Malta
Singapore
Sri Lanka
Trinidad & Tobago
Zimbabwe

HONORARY REPRESENTATIVES [18]

Antigua
BAOR
Barbados
Brunei
Cayman Islands
Cyprus
Fiji
India
Kenya
Malawi
Mauritius
Nigeria
St Lucia
Seychelles
Solomon Islands
Tanzania
Uganda
Zambia

OVERSEA EXAMINERS [14]

Bahrain
Bangladesh
Botswana
Canary Islands
Cook Islands
Falkland Islands
Indonesia
Papua New Guinea
Saudi Arabia
Sierra Leone
Sudan
Sultanate of Oman
United Arab Emirates
Vanuatu

COMMONWEALTH COUNCIL – 1990

THE ROYAL LIFE SAVING SOCIETY

Founded in 1891 incorporated by Royal Charter
Registered Charity No 306094

Patron:
HER MAJESTY THE QUEEN

Commonwealth President:
HIS ROYAL HIGHNESS
PRINCE MICHAEL OF KENT

Deputy Commonwealth President:
SIR ROBIN GILLETT Bt GBE RD

Commonwealth Council Representatives:

AUSTRALIA
HE The Hon Douglas McClelland AC
Neville Bayfield
Geoffrey S Large

CANADA
HE The Hon Donald Macdonald PC
Judy Kent
Raymond T Vaudry

NEW ZEALAND
HE Mr Bryce Harland
J Allen Lee
Norman A Morris QSM

UNITED KINGDOM
Brian Weigh CBE QPM
Brian Morrissey OBE QPM
Anthony J Handley

HONORARY TREASURER
Jack G Wilson

CHIEF COMMONWEALTH SECRETARY
John W R Taylor

APPENDIX 2

MOUNTBATTEN MEDAL WINNERS

1951 ROBERT B. WARDLE of CANADA
1952 SALLY ELWIN JUPP of Enfield, Middlesex, ENGLAND
1953 MRS SYBIL HIGGINS of Culleenamore, County Sligo, NORTHERN IRELAND
1954 FRANCIS KOH TECK CHONG of Klang, MALAYA
1955 FREDERICK POTGIETER and NEVILLE G. MAIER of SOUTH AFRICA
1956 BERNARD LITWACK of Southport, Lancashire, ENGLAND
1957 PETER CRITCHLEY of Cheadle, Cheshire, ENGLAND
1958 DUNCAN McLEAN CAMPBELL of Fulham, London, ENGLAND
1959 PC 483 RICHARD COOKE, Nottingham City Police, ENGLAND
1960 DAVID TAYLOR of Preston, Lancashire, ENGLAND
1961 DENNIS J. McLELLAN of New South Wales, AUSTRALIA
1962 HILARY WESTERMAN of Leeds, Yorkshire, ENGLAND
1963 KENNETH D. HOWLETT of Edmonton, CANADA
1964 LYNDA R. DANN of Alberta, CANADA
1965 TERRENCE H. SCORER of WESTERN AUSTRALIA
1966 JACK M. EASTON of Forfar, SCOTLAND
1967 MANASA K. VATULOKA of FIJI
1968 BARRY J. McNEIL of Auckland, NEW ZEALAND
1969 RONALD M. HESLOP of Stirling, SCOTLAND
1970 MRS D. PATRICIA POPE of Wakefield, Yorkshire, ENGLAND
1971 K .GRANT ROBSON of New South Wales, AUSTRALIA
1972 DAVID J. ROWE of Devon, ENGLAND
1973 not awarded
1974 BERNARD W. ROBINS of Devon, ENGLAND
1975 GORDON PENNER of CANADA
1976 PATRICK McMAHON of Limerick, NORTHERN IRELAND
1977 MRS PAULINE A. MacLEAN of Hamilton, SCOTLAND
1978 GEORGE GEDDES PARSONAGE of Glasgow, SCOTLAND
1979 PATRICK MARIE BERNARD FARGE of Whangarei, NEW ZEALAND
1980 JOHN POTTS of Omagh, NORTHERN IRELAND
1981 EVAN FRANKLIN DAVIES of Rhyl, WALES
1982 KENNETH JOHN RAYNOR of Nottingham, ENGLAND
1983 PC PATRICK RICHARD ABRAM, Lancashire Constabulary, ENGLAND
1984 not awarded
1985 HOLLY JACQUELINE PHILLIPS, Richmond, Surrey, ENGLAND
1986 not awarded
1987 not awarded
1988 PENNY CLAYTON, Dunedin, NEW ZEALAND

BIBLIOGRAPHY

This is the first book devoted to lifesaving, although lifesaving material can be found in books and magazines relating to swimming and first aid. I therefore am grateful to the Royal Life Saving Society for giving me access to their archives and their marvellous range of textbooks and manuals. The archives contain admirable and closely researched material written by members.

Books by the RLSS UK include:

Aquatic Lifesaving for Supervisors of People with Disabilities
Lifeguard Manual
Lifesaving
Pool Lifeguarding
Resuscitation and First Aid
Teaching Water Safety: A Project Approach

Among the most interesting and informative of books not produced by the RLSS are the following:

Besford, P. *Encyclopaedia of Swimming* ,1971
Kay, James. *How to Teach Swimming*, 1901
Oppenheim, F. *The History of Swimming*, 1970
Sinclair, Archibald and Henry, William. *Swimming*, 1901
Thomas, Ralph *Swimming*, 1904

Early magazines such as *The Swimmer, Swimming, Swimming Magazine, English Sport,* have proved to contain much interesting material relating to the early days of the Royal Life Saving Society.

Ronald Pearsall

INDEX

ROYAL LIFE SAVING SOCIETY